CANOEING WITH JOSÉ

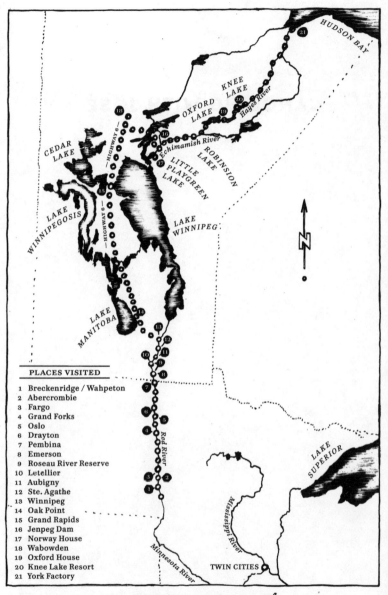

PLACES VISITED

1 Breckenridge / Wahpeton
2 Abercrombie
3 Fargo
4 Grand Forks
5 Oslo
6 Drayton
7 Pembina
8 Emerson
9 Roseau River Reserve
10 Letellior
11 Aubigny
12 Ste. Agathe
13 Winnipeg
14 Oak Point
15 Grand Rapids
16 Jenpeg Dam
17 Norway House
18 Wabowden
19 Oxford House
20 Knee Lake Resort
21 York Factory

CANOEING WITH JOSÉ

CANOEING WITH JOSÉ

JON LURIE

GV782.42.L87 A3 2017
Lurie, Jon, 1967- author.
Canoeing with Jos
Minneapolis, Minnesota :
Milkweed Editions, 2017.

Published 2017 by Milkweed Editions
Printed in the United States of America
Cover and text design by Adam B. Bohannon
Cover photo by Jon Lurie
Author photo by Aoife Roberts
Frontispiece map by Nate Christopherson and Karl Engebretson
17 18 19 20 21   5 4 3 2 1
First Edition

Milkweed Editions, an independent nonprofit publisher, gratefully acknowledges sustaining support from the Jerome Foundation; the Lindquist & Vennum Foundation; the McKnight Foundation; the National Endowment for the Arts; the Target Foundation; and other generous contributions from foundations, corporations, and individuals. Also, this activity is made possible by the voters of Minnesota through a Minnesota State Arts Board Operating Support grant, thanks to a legislative appropriation from the arts and cultural heritage fund, and a grant from the Wells Fargo Foundation. For a full listing of Milkweed Editions supporters, please visit milkweed.org.

Library of Congress Cataloging-in-Publication Data
Names: Lurie, Jon, 1967- author.
Title: Canoeing with José / Jon Lurie.
Description: Minneapolis, Minnesota : Milkweed Editions, 2017.
Identifiers: LCCN 2017000234 | ISBN 9781571313218 (paperback)
Subjects: LCSH: Lurie, Jon, 1967---Travel--Red River of the North. | Canoes and canoeing--Red River of the North. | Red River of the North--Description and travel. | BISAC: BIOGRAPHY & AUTOBIOGRAPHY / Personal Memoirs. | SPORTS & RECREATION / Canoeing. | BIOGRAPHY & AUTOBIOGRAPHY / Native Americans. | SPORTS & RECREATION / Camping.
Classification: LCC GV782.42.L87 A3 2017 | DDC 797.12209784/1--dc23
LC record available at https://lccn.loc.gov/2017000234

Milkweed Editions is committed to ecological stewardship. We strive to align our book production practices with this principle, and to reduce the impact of our operations in the environment. We are a member of the Green Press Initiative, a nonprofit coalition of publishers, manufacturers, and authors working to protect the world's endangered forests and conserve natural resources. *Canoeing with José* was printed on acid-free 100% postconsumer-waste paper by Edwards Brothers Malloy.

*For Allison, Chaske, Edmond, Gemma, José, Lillieannah,
Malcolm, Mariah, and Martha*

CONTENTS

A NOTE ON THE USE OF LAKOTA, DAKOTA, AND SIOUX

José has both Lakota and Dakota ancestry on his mother's side. The Lakota and Dakota are divisions of the Oceti Sakowin Oyate (Seven Fires Nation), or Sioux, the name given them by early French traders. The Dakota and Lakota people speak different dialects of the same language and share many cultural and spiritual traditions. Today the Dakota people's homelands are located primarily in Minnesota and the eastern Dakotas, while the Lakota are settled primarily in western South Dakota. José uses Lakota, Dakota, and Sioux to describe his ethnicity, but does not use them interchangeably. He asserts one or the other branch of his Native heritage depending upon the topic and to whom he is speaking.

PROLOGUE

As a child I spent hours alone, roaming the woods near my home on the western edge of Minneapolis. I often dug my hands into the dank soil, praying to find an arrowhead, a piece of pottery, a handwritten note—some kind of clue that would help me understand who I was, where I was.

I had always been intrigued by the waterways around me, and by their names. But because my family was not of Minnesota, was not Dakota, no one ever told me that *mni* means "water." *Mni* is embedded in the names of many places in Minnesota (Land of Smoky Waters): Minneapolis (City of Water), small towns like Minnewasta (Beautiful Waters) and Minneota (Abundant Waters), and giant lakes like Minnetonka (Great Waters). From the Minnesota River in the south to Big Stone Lake in the west, and from the Rainy River in the north to the St. Croix River in the east, water pulses through the arteries of the region I grew up in.

I remember one summer morning as an early crystallization of my lifelong love of the waterways of Minnesota.

I was eight years old, just a few weeks from entering third grade. While playing at a park called Twin Lakes, I noticed a stand of golden cattails along the edge of a baseball diamond, waving at me like old friends across the manicured outfield. I wandered away from the teenager whom my mother had often charged with my care that summer. As I reached for a velveteen bloom atop a cattail's spindly stock, I slipped into the marsh. Black mud and swamp water crept up to my knees, and then, clawing against slick banks, I quickly slid neck-deep into the muskeg. I turned toward the narrow band of open water that snaked through the cattails and swam, struggling through the rushes. Before long the sky opened and I emerged into a pond. I recognized it as the same pond where my little brother and I shoveled snow and played hockey in the winter. And with this recognition came a realization: Twin Lakes Park, which had always seemed so far away, was connected by water to this known place.

I blazed a trail through the pond's copious green algae, swam around a buoy, and pulled myself up onto the grassy shore. After catching my breath, I wanted to know where the water flowed next. I noticed in one boggy corner a culvert, which ran beneath Cedarwood Road. I had seen this concrete tunnel many times from the road. I had even stood on it, skipping rocks. But until this afternoon, I had never wondered what it was for.

I walked along the shore to the culvert and observed the gurgling inflow. It occurred to me that this was the water's next pathway, underground through this pipe. I followed it across a series of wooded backyards, tracking an old streambed to where the water surfaced again through the grated end of the concrete tube. The creek flowed lazily to the east and then entered another dark, whispering tunnel. From its entrance, I could see the windows of my bedroom.

My siblings and I had always referred to this patch of woods as the "creek." We played there, built dams and rapids, swimming holes and forts. Deer occasionally happened through. This was one of the places where I dug in the earth, searching for clues.

I roamed the woods along the creek for weeks after this accidental adventure, but I was unable to locate the far end of that last dark tunnel. Finally, I inflated a small air mattress and floated into the tube. The water was shallow, and I pushed along the cold stone walls until I spilled into a wetland along France Avenue.

I quickly recognized this as the spot where my four older sisters and I flew kites in dry seasons. I could see the upper floors of the IDS Center, Minneapolis's newest skyscraper, rising above the treetops and reflecting the aqua sky. I abandoned my raft and, following the trajectory of another culvert, walked over Basswood Road. I stood on the western shore of Cedar Lake and watched as water from the tube—water that had begun its journey at least three miles away, in Twin Lakes Park—flowed into the calm blue. I took in the open water, breathing deeply.

In subsequent expeditions that summer, I pedaled my Schwinn Stingray around Cedar Lake, eventually reaching the opposite shore, where I came upon a canal. I stood on a railroad bridge spanning the canal and looked down at the water. Had I continued to the next links in the Minneapolis Chain, I would have come first to Lake of the Isles, then to Lake Calhoun, and on to Lake Harriet. From there I would have found my way to Minnehaha Creek, and then on to the gateway to the world, the Mississippi River, which flows from Minnesota to the Gulf of Mexico.

I can still envision the sunlight filtering down through the towering red cedars and swaying willows that lined the canal. As a child observing this waterway for the first time, I ached to follow it. To be like the water, which always traveled but was never lost.

CANOEING WITH JOSÉ

THE SEVAREID LIBRARY

When I catch wind of a newsworthy story, I feel like a burning man seeking water, driven to hit the road and investigate. I have experienced this compulsion repeatedly, working as a freelance journalist for magazines and newspapers across North America. It has motivated me to cover stories from Canada to Mexico, and from Washington, DC, to the Alaskan Arctic. But the first time it happened was in September 1988, weeks after the start of my first semester at the University of Minnesota.

The initial spark occurred when I took in a speech at Coffman Memorial Union. The speaker was a fiery Nicaraguan, a Sandinista rebel with a red beret. She railed against abuses inflicted upon Central Americans at the border. "The United States is starting wars against democratically elected governments in Central America," she proclaimed. "The American government is backing violent dictatorial regimes and then imprisoning the individuals who arrive at the border seeking simple human dignity."

Intending to write a paper based on this talk for my History of Civil Rights class, I scribbled notes on a yellow legal pad. The speaker was deadly earnest—the way people are when they've experienced war. And when she referred to the detention centers that had popped up in Texas as concentration camps, I knew I had to go.

My grandmother, Paulette Oppert, had lost a husband to the Nazis, placed her children (including my mother) in hiding during the occupation of France, and seen trainloads of Jews deported to the East. *Maman* had always taught me that my greatest responsibility was to remain vigilant against genocide. I was on this Earth above all, she often told me, to help make certain there was never another Holocaust. To this end, she had always encouraged me to write, and to keep a gun in the house.

Three days after hearing the Sandinista speak, I set out for the Rio Grande River Valley, 1500 miles south of Minneapolis. As I accelerated onto Interstate 35, blasting punk rock mixtapes, I felt as if I were finding my destiny. I had interviewed *Maman* extensively over the years, and I intended to write her biography. After years of searching for an identity, and having exprienced dozens of instances of anti-Semitism myself, I had settled on a personal narrative based on my grandparents' involvement in the French Resistance. Maquis members served as guerilla fighters, underground newspaper publishers, and manufacturers of forged government documents. They fought alongside the American and British soldiers who liberated France from the Nazis. As I headed for the American concentration camps, I finally had a mission that paralleled this history.

Back home in Minneapolis after a week on the road, I submitted a 5000-word story to the professor who taught my History of Civil Rights course. He encouraged me to publish it, and so I addressed a copy to Steven Lorinser, editor in chief of the student-produced *Minnesota Daily*. I was ecstatic when he phoned to arrange a meeting.

I found Lorinser waiting for me at a secluded table in the Eric Sevareid Journalism Library. He was dressed in slacks, loafers, and a crisp shirt. His hair was neatly parted on the side and he comported himself like a professional. My head was shaved and I showed up in Chuck Taylors, a tattered sweatshirt, and frayed jeans.

Lorinser was impressed with the reporting I had done from Texas, and asked about my other interests. He called me gutsy, committed to printing my story in the *Daily*, and promised more opportunities for me to write for the paper.

I described my backpacking journeys in South America and Europe, and the extensive road trips I'd taken to every corner of the United States. As we talked, we discovered a shared love of the Northwoods and canoeing. I told him I'd spent five consecutive summers at a canoe camp on the Canadian border as a teenager, culminating in a 30-day paddle across northern Ontario. I went on to explain how those experiences had led to employment guiding youth on canoe and backpacking trips.

Lorinser's face lit up like a match to birch bark. He asked if I knew of a book called *Canoeing with the Cree*.

I shook my head.

"It was actually written by that guy," he said, pointing to a bust in the middle of the library. He went on to explain how Eric Sevareid had paddled from Minneapolis to Hudson Bay with his friend Walter Port, a distance of some 2300 miles. They undertook the expedition when they were just 17 and 19 years old.

After the journey, Lorinser continued, Sevareid graduated from the University of Minnesota, and went on to become one of Edward R. Murrow's courageous correspondents, the first to report on the fall of Paris to Nazi forces in June 1940. When I learned that Sevareid had been denied the editor in chief position at the *Daily* following a controversial column he'd written in 1934, my admiration for him was boundless. And according to Lorinser, *Canoeing with the Cree* was his first published work.

I pumped Lorinser for details of Sevareid and Port's route, astonished that there was a passage by waterway from Minnesota to Hudson Bay. But it had been years since he read the memoir, and he couldn't recall much more than he'd told me already.

Animated by the exchange, Lorinser and I searched the Sevareid Library for a copy of *Canoeing with the Cree*. According to the card catalog, the book should have been shelved and available. But apparently I wasn't the only one interested in this audacious trip.

We queried a librarian, who smiled unexpectedly. She called the book "a regional classic" and "Minnesota's version of Huck Finn," before apologizing sheepishly for the missing volume. "Some people forget to sign it out," she explained, and then suggested that I check the university bookstore.

I hurried across campus and found a short stack of tan paperbacks on the "Minnesota Interest" table, surrounded by books on Vikings football greats, classic hot dish recipes, and the Twin Cities' best fishing holes. The cover featured a photograph of a strapping Sevareid wearing baggy pants tucked into knee-high boots and a button-up khaki shirt, posing jauntily with hands on his hips. He could have passed for a Mountie, and he appeared to be at least 30 years old.

At the time, I was living in a dingy apartment above the CC Club. Every night the seedy Uptown tavern was crowded with punks, hipsters, and blue-collar regulars drinking Grain Belt from plastic pitchers and listening to the jukebox—a catalog of the thriving punk scene that pulsed on the streets of Minneapolis's south side. Many of the musicians playing on these records were CC regulars: Grant Hart from Hüsker Dü, Bob Stinson from the Replacements, members of Soul Asylum, Blue Hippos, Run Westy Run, and Babes in Toyland.

I was generally seething at the state of the world, and when the jukebox rumbled with livid punk rock, crackling the linoleum tile on the kitchen floor until well after midnight, it resonated like the beat of my heart. But on the cool October night when I returned home from campus with a copy of *Canoeing with the Cree*, I longed for silence.

Had I judged the book by its cover, or by its opening lines, I would have rejected *Canoeing with the Cree* immediately. While I was just a few weeks into my first Native American studies class and my awareness of the history and culture of Minnesota's indigenous people was still embryonic, I knew enough to dismiss the cover copy's assertion that Sevareid and Port were the first to paddle from Minnesota to Hudson Bay. Given the long history of Native peoples and voyageurs traversing the vast system of waterways extending from the mouth of the St. Lawrence River to Hudson Bay and the Great Lakes, I was confident that this journey had been undertaken long before Sevareid and Port. Nor was I particularly impressed by the citation from Kipling that begins the first chapter, with its reference to "Red Gods making their medicine."

As I turned the pages of *Canoeing with the Cree* that first time, however, I suspended judgment on the book's grandiose claims, and on the racist attitude of its author. After all, when Sevareid and Port made their journey in 1930, indigenous people had only been granted American citizenship for six years (the Indian Citizenship Act having passed in 1924), their religious practices were strictly outlawed, and their culture had been decimated by government policies that forced thousands of Native children into boarding schools, where they were held away from their families, made to dress like white people, and severely punished for speaking their languages.

Instead, I read *Canoeing with the Cree* that first time as

an adventure story. I burned to know the boys' route. After launching at the confluence of the Minnesota and Mississippi Rivers in Saint Paul, they had paddled up the Minnesota River and its tributary, the Little Minnesota River, to Browns Valley, Minnesota. From there, the boys portaged over the Laurentian Divide to Lake Traverse and descended the Bois des Sioux River to the Red River of the North, which led to Lake Winnipeg. Then they had paddled down the Nelson River, across a series of small lakes and portages to Gods River, and down the Hayes River to York Factory on Hudson Bay.

Canoeing with the Cree supplied me with something I had never experienced: a homegrown mythology. Theirs was not the tale of 17th-century voyageurs paddling 600-pound Montreal freighter canoes on the Great Lakes, nor the Anishinaabe's sacred migration from the mouth of the Saint Lawrence through the Great Lakes to the *land where food grows on the water*. Sevareid and Port had grown up in a neighborhood less than five miles from my own and sought adventure in a used canvas canoe. They had embraced an ambitious vision and found the nerve to follow the water.

When I turned the last page of this extraordinary tale, the floor pulsing beneath me, I silently declared my intention to retrace their path to Hudson Bay as soon as possible. Little did I know that it would be 15 years before I realized this dream.

The spring of 2002 was brutal. I had lost my editorial job in Alaska, and it was obvious that my marriage of 13 years was swirling down the drain. I was 34 years old, and I decided to return to Minneapolis to write for the Native newspaper where my career in journalism had begun a decade before.

Over the course of the previous decade, my work for *The Circle*, *Indian Country Today*, the *Sicangu Sun-Times*, and other Native publications had led me to places and provided me with experiences accessible to few white people. I had met and befriended Native elders and philosophers, professors and activists, medicine men and political leaders. I had participated in Lakota ceremonies and learned from ordinary tribal citizens in cities and on reservations, from Rosebud to Pine Ridge, and from Arctic Village to White Earth, Upper and Lower Sioux, Isleta Pueblo, Bad River, and many others. These experiences had taken me far from my upbringing in a conservative Jewish household in Minneapolis, fulfilling in many ways what I longed for as a young man: to live a deeply meaningful life connected with the land of my birth. I had also come to understand the extent to which mainstream Americans were beneficiaries of the genocide of indigenous peoples, and it didn't sit well with me. It never had, even when I was too young to know why.

In addition to reporting, *The Circle* had hired me to teach in their youth journalism program. I met José on the first day of the summer session, at *The Circle*'s office in south Minneapolis. He was sitting at a desk with two other interns, eyeing me suspiciously from beneath a powder-blue baseball cap. The program director introduced me, running down a list of my accomplishments: several hundred published articles in over two dozen papers and magazines, three nonfiction children's books, 12 years reporting in Native American communities, and a brief tenure as the editor in chief of Alaska's second-largest newspaper.

José kicked his Adidas up onto the table and leaned back in his chair. He yanked at a silver pistol that hung from a chain around his neck, and raised his hand as if saluting the Führer.

"Yes?" I nodded.

"Got just one question. Why they had to get some Nazi up in here to mess with our writing? You ever read *New Voices*? It says right there on the cover, *The Voice of Native Youth*. By the looks of things, you ain't knowing a damn thing about Native youth."

José's hostility didn't surprise me. I used his charge as an opening.

"I'm no Nazi," I replied. "I'm a Jew. The only reason I'm

in this country is because Hitler tried to kill my people in Europe. And I'm not here to mess with your writing. I'm here to help you say whatever you want to say."

José pulled his feet off the table and let them land with a thud. "You tryna say you down and all that, tryna come off like you 'bout it? First off, I don't need no editor. At Heart of the Earth Survival School, I'm the editor of the school paper. And I don't need no thought police stepping on my First Amendment rights."

The program director glanced at the clock. "It's time to get working on your stories. Each of you will take a turn working with Jon. Who's ready to go first?"

José stood, his bravado bolder than his lanky frame would suggest. "I'll go. Ain't no one gonna fuck with my shit." He breathed up at my chin, then swaggered into the conference room with a cherry iBook under his arm.

José set the computer on the mahogany table and opened the lid. "You can't say nothing 'bout this. You gotsta be down with the hip-hop game before you can say word one."

A document titled "Ja Rule and 50 Cent Leave Blood on the Tracks" filled the screen. As I read the article, it became clear that this was José's commentary on the latest feud between rival hip-hop artists. Such conflicts had led to the murders of some of rap music's biggest stars in recent months.

José pulled a butterfly knife from his back pocket and whipped it around above his head like a rodeo ninja. "What can you even say? You ain't down with the game, the youth, the Native Americans."

"These gangstas gots to be bigger than that," he wrote. "They gots to leave the beef char-broiling at Burger King and stick to making dope records. We all remember those who been felled by the bullet: Biggie Smalls, Tupac Shakur, and Notorious BIG. But ain't nothing ever gonna bring 'em back. We can't afford to lose no more of our voices from the ghetto to senseless murder and mayhem. I got a message for all you rhyme-slingers out there thinking you badder than Ice-T in NWA: Leave the damn blood on the tracks."

I was impressed with the piece. José was writing in the language of hip-hop. He had a clear sense of intended audience. And he was good with metaphor.

There were some glaring factual errors that I hoped to take up with him, but in the meantime, the verbal battery went on. "You gotsta have street cred ta fuck with my shit. Man, they'd tear your punk ass up on the mothafuckin' block."

"You little bitch," I interjected. "I was listening to rap music while you were still shitting your diapers." I was genuinely irritated, but I was also taking a calculated risk. When I lived on the Rosebud Reservation I had worked part-time as a substitute teacher, and I quickly learned that one way to win the respect of a streetwise teen was to get in his face.

Occasionally, though, the strategy backfired.

José wasn't laughing. He jumped out of his chair and stood over me, butterfly knife resting at his hip. "You calling me a little bitch?'

"That's right," I said. "Professionals understand that editing is part of the business."

"You little bitch," José hissed back at me. He put his hands on a long aluminum cabinet that stood against the wall by the door, then lowered his head and went silent.

The sudden hush worried me, and I took a more conciliatory tack.

"Come over here and sit down," I said. "Let me show you how a few small changes could improve your article." I scrolled down a page on the iBook. "In the final paragraph, where you say Ice-T was in NWA? He was never in NWA. You must have been thinking of Ice Cube."

José pushed off the cabinet and clapped like a boxer doing push-ups.

"And here, where you list the names of the rappers who have been murdered: Notorious B.I.G., Tupac Shakur, and Biggie Smalls? That's not right. It's true they were murdered, but Biggie Smalls and Notorious B.I.G. were the same guy."

José's cheeks went scarlet, and he squealed in falsetto, "Whaaat?"

"Fact checking–"

"Whaaat?" he sang out again, then bounced his backside off the aluminum cabinet. It rocked against the wall and tilted forward. The doors swung open and office supplies crashed to the floor.

"What the fuck," José yelped, dancing out of the way. He tripped on a cardboard box, stumbled over a chair, and fell to the floor, surrounded by ink pads, manila envelopes, and computer cords.

He ignored my help, pushed himself to his knees, and rifled through the debris.

His knife was missing, replaced in his right hand by a long eagle-feather ink stamp he had uncovered among the office supplies. A group project from days gone by, the stamp was made from a rectangle of rough-edged steel. I saw beside it a shallow ink pad encased in tin.

"Let's do those changes you came up with, dawg. But hit me with this first." José rubbed the rectangular stamp in black ink and handed it to me.

"Hit me!" He slapped his sinewy left shoulder, flexing. "Do it!"

I took a breath and jabbed the stamp home. When I pulled back, an eagle-feather tattoo appeared near the top of José's shoulder.

"Now you, dawg," he giggled, smothering the stamp in ink.

I rolled up my sleeve and flexed.

José took three giant steps backward. "Hang on. I'm gonna do this."

He ran at me, the stamp cocked above his head, and

brought it down on my shoulder, the sharp corner piercing my flesh.

I doubled over in pain. "What the hell!"

I pulled tentatively at the gash on my shoulder. My eagle feather was smeared, the black ink mingling with bright blood. It hurt, but I also felt relief as a red stream wound down my arm.

José beamed at his handiwork, and after a second of hesitation, we laughed together like maniacs.

FORT SNELLING SPECTERS

In the spring of 2006, several years after my initial encounter with José, I was in a very bad way. I had recently lost my wife of 13 years to a divorce, a young friend to brain cancer, and my beloved *Maman* to the inevitable march of time. The sick cinema in my head played a continuous loop of rage and self-pity. I had begun crying late the previous year, and I couldn't stop.

I was ashamed that my four kids had to see me in such a wretched state, but even as I resolved to get a grip—seeing therapists, exhausting friendships, and self-medicating—I remained prisoner to a vicious depression. And when panic attacked late at night, I often called José, who had become a trusted friend.

"Bro," I would groan, feigning a laugh, "I'm mentally ill."

Our roles had reversed. In the early stages of our friendship, I had fielded the late-night calls. José called me from a juvenile detention center after he was arrested for stealing cars. He called to ask if he could borrow money when his grandmother's supply of heating oil was cut off in the winter, and when he needed to be bailed out of jail after smashing a liquor bottle over the head of his mother's abusive boyfriend. And he called when he was expelled from high school for engaging in gang activity.

"You're not mentally ill," José would reply. "If you were, you wouldn't be able to laugh about it."

Regardless of the wisdom of this assertion, I couldn't overcome the crippling pain that wretched spring. And then one night I received a phone call around 3:00 a.m.

I didn't get the details immediately—José was frantic, talking a mile a minute—but later I put together what had happened. José had been at Regions Hospital, where his girlfriend, Joan, was giving birth. Joan is Anishinaabe, and José is Lakota and Puerto Rican. When the baby was born black, José was the last person in the room to realize he couldn't possibly be the father. After he cut the umbilical cord, a nurse grabbed his wrist and snipped off the hospital bracelet. No one in the delivery room had the compassion to stop him as he ran out in a state of shock, determined to murder the crack dealer who had likely impregnated Joan.

I immediately agreed to take José in. Neither of us slept that first night, but we were out the door by 9:00 a.m. It was a bleak morning in early April, and we drove the labyrinth of one-way streets in downtown Saint Paul, a pair of zombies looking for the Ramsey County Vital Records office.

José's grandmother had charged him with filing a series of documents enjoining their Mahpiya Zi (Yellow Cloud) clan to a lawsuit related to the US-Dakota War of 1862. There were casino fortunes at stake for Dakota people who could prove their ancestors' loyalty to the United States during the war. And so a century and a half after the Dakota were rounded up by Colonel Henry Sibley's army, imprisoned at Fort Snelling, loaded onto Mississippi steamboats in Saint Paul, and forcibly exiled from Minnesota, José had until midnight to register a claim.

Contrary to the gist of the documents, however, José's great-grandfather could hardly be called a loyalist. In fact, he was among the 38 Dakota men hanged along the banks of the Minnesota River for defending his people. José knew his family's claim to loyalty was fraudulent and he was disgusted by it. But he also understood their desire for reparations. After all, the Dakota had been treated unjustly for generations.

"My great-grandfather was convicted of killing white settlers, so hell no, we ain't loyal. I'd rather have my history than some bullshit casino money. But the rest of the family don't give a fuck," he sniffed.

I pulled to the curb outside the building that housed the Vital Records office. José stepped out of the car and blazed a Cool Menthol in the raw morning air. He looked at me through the window opening. "I'm gonna kill that fucking whore and that nigger crackhead."

I was used to José throwing the term "nigga" around. Where I was from any variation of the n-word meant the same thing, and its use was strictly taboo. But over time I had come to understand that "nigga" was used on the streets the same way a middle-class white kid might say dude, buddy, or homeboy. When José finished the word with the hard *r* in this case, however, I knew it meant something else altogether. This was racial, hateful, and ugly.

I made a feeble attempt to admonish him: "The color of his skin had nothing to do with it." But the words sounded absurd in the face of his rage, and José turned away dismissively.

Just two weeks before the demoralizing revelation in the maternity ward, José had asked me to curtail the late-night calls for help. "Look," he murmured with gentle authority during one of the last such exchanges, "we're winding down around here. Just got the boy to bed, and I have to work in the morning." Joan and her first child had moved into José's basement apartment in Henry Sibley Manor, the notorious housing projects off West 7th Street in Saint Paul. He was planning to marry her and adopt the two-year-old as his son.

José emerged from the Vital Records office minutes later, gripping his birth certificate. He slumped onto the passenger seat and folded the paper, then placed it inside an envelope containing his family members' tribal documents and a blank family tree.

We drove to a taqueria and ordered burritos. I filled in the empty branches on the family tree while José scratched his head and recalled what he knew of his family's story.

His grandparents, his mother, and her five sisters were

from the Rosebud Indian Reservation in South Dakota. José spent his early years in Chicago, where the family had settled in the early seventies as part of a government relocation program. His father was a Puerto Rican gang member, a Dragon Disciple, who died from a cocaine overdose when José was 15 years old, the same year I met him at *The Circle*.

José's mother met his father on the streets of Chicago's West Side. José learned at a very young age not to mess with her. "My mom used to do armed robberies for the Latin Queens," he once told me. "She was homicidal, bro." Unlike many of his cousins, who endured painful initiations as teens, José was born into gang life.

In the early eighties, José's family migrated north to Saint Paul in an effort to escape the violence that was spiraling out of control in Chicago. It was a time when many men of his father's generation were claimed by violence, drugs, alcohol, and the criminal justice system.

By the time he was a freshman in high school, José was doing his best to feed his six brothers and sisters. He bought his first eight-ball of crack (3.5 grams) at 14, and started selling it on the streets of Saint Paul's Frogtown neighborhood, which was known in those days as Cracktown.

José squirted red sauce from packets onto his tortilla, then switched the subject from his family history to a budding scheme to murder Joan and Sonic. I assumed he meant it, and intended to keep him under wing until his sleep-deprived delirium subsided. Grinding his teeth and gazing out at the cars passing on Snelling Avenue, he added, "I think I'm going to fucking explode if I don't cry. I haven't been able to since my dad died. I just wish I could cry."

I shuttled José to my bank to get his documents notarized, then across town to the post office at the airport. I drove slowly and took the long way, down Shepherd Road, along the high bluffs of the Mississippi River Gorge, and across the bridge connecting Saint Paul to Minneapolis at Historic Fort Snelling, a US Army post originally constructed in the 1830s. As we crossed the bridge, I looked down to the glistening intersection of the Mississippi and Minnesota Rivers at Pike Island, the very spot where Eric Sevareid and Walter Port had set out on their epic journey to Hudson Bay on June 17, 1930. This area, known to the Dakota as Bdote, is a sacred site, the setting for one of their creation stories.

I had long thought of that opening in the forest canopy as a secret passageway out of my life. Since discovering *Canoeing with the Cree* in college, I had dreamed of replicating the 2250-mile route. As they often did when I drove across that span, the specters of Sevareid and Port swung their 18-foot canvas canoe around the tip of Pike Island and headed into the languorous current of the Minnesota River. I imagined myself down there with them now, in the stern of the *Sans Souci*, paddling so hard the ache began to drain from my chest.

Lost in this reverie, I almost veered off the bridge. José

barely flinched, raising an eyebrow under the cocked rim of his black-on-black Minnesota Twins cap.

I had never mentioned Sevareid and Port's journey to José. I suppose I didn't think he would be interested in the exploits of a couple of white kids. Nor did I see him as the kind of guy who would undertake a canoe expedition. And in any case, it all seemed trivial compared to what he was going through.

I called José's attention to the river bottoms beneath Fort Snelling, pointing out the swamp that once contained a concentration camp where more than 1700 of his Dakota ancestors—men, women, and children—spent the miserable winter of 1862–1863. Over the course of that one harsh season, some 300 Dakota died from malnutrition, disease, and exposure.

It had always bothered me that this ghastly chapter in Minnesota's history is not noted in Sevareid's account, even though he and Port launched their expedition from that blood-stained plot beneath Fort Snelling only a few decades after the atrocities took place. Now, José seemed astounded to learn that his people's nightmare had taken place in the shadow of the historic fort he had visited on school field trips.

"I ain't gonna lie, dawg," he said earnestly, "that's some fucked-up shit."

Later that day, around midnight, fatigue overtook rage. José's eyes rolled like greased marbles under swollen lids as we sat in the living room of my apartment. My kids were with their mother that night, freeing me to smoke weed while he downed Coronas.

Eventually I showed José to my bedroom, gave him one of my antianxiety pills, and demanded the Chinese fighting knives he carried in his waistband.

He handed them over reluctantly.

"Gotsta have those knives, bro," he said, following me into the kitchen. "I ain't about to walk the streets without them."

When I questioned his need to bring the weapons to bed, he replied flatly, "Sometimes I gotsta back some motherfuckers off."

I assured him I would double-check the locks, and provide protection while he slept. He hovered nearby as I set the ornate chrome blades in the cupboard above the sink. Then we both crashed.

I awoke on the couch just before dawn. I lay listening to the thump of my heart, feeling my blood pulse like acid through my body. I flipped on the light in the bathroom. My cheeks were lined and my eyes subsumed in puffy sockets. In the past four months I had lost 25 pounds, and I looked as if I had aged five years.

I lay back down and stayed there, excruciatingly aware of the crescent moon slicing the jagged rooftops across the street until sunrise. It was then that I heard José tiptoe down the stairs. He paused at the edge of the couch, seemingly surprised to find my eyes open. He complained that he hadn't slept, then went to the kitchen cupboard, jammed the Chinese fighting knives into the waistband of his jeans, and headed for the front door.

I knew José was lying when he claimed he was "funna bus it home, back to the crib to get a clean 'fit." Even after a terrible night, his Enyce shirt was nicely pressed, and his jeans still held the pleats he had ironed in the day before.

I insisted on driving him home.

As we glided silently to Sibley Manor, it was increasingly clear to me that José was about to make a life-altering mistake. When we arrived outside his building, he tried to slip away quickly. "Alright then, dawg," he said, pulling the door handle.

"Are you coming back?" I asked.

He pulled his leg inside, clicked the door shut, and spoke with surprising directness. "The people I'm from, we use violence to settle things. It's just the way it is. What we know."

I threw his logic back at him. "You're not crazy if you know you're crazy. You don't have to do that. You can forgive Joan."

José paused, then admitted that he still loved Joan. But, he added, he would never be able to forgive her.

"You knew Joan had a thing with Sonic when you two were split up, and a couple nights ago you still loved her enough to marry her," I said. "If you really loved her then, you would still love her now."

José took this in silently. He wondered aloud if Joan might agree to give up "that little *hasapa*," Lakota slang for a black baby. Then he asked to use my phone to call her.

Joan answered.

José said he loved her and needed to talk. He said he could forgive her, and wanted to try again. His apparent transformation from juvenile thug to mature young man was convincing. I drove off from Sibley Manor believing him, a state of delusion that would last until he appeared at my door a few nights later, out of breath and trembling.

He explained quickly that he had just sprinted across Interstate 94 from Frogtown, after "blasting that Sonic motherfucker with a sawed-off." I would later learn that he had waited for Sonic outside Joan's mother's house, where she and the baby were staying. When Sonic appeared, José shot out the rear window of his Oldsmobile 98.

I pulled José into my apartment, looked up and down the street, and bolted the door.

OLD HAL AND HAWK'S CANOE

The nights following this drama with José were stormy, with violent winds that lulled me to sleep the way unsettled weather always has. I didn't hear much from him after the night he went after Sonic and crashed at my place, and I prayed that no news was good news.

In the meantime, I had decided that I was going to Hudson Bay, and José had agreed to join me. Planning for the expedition was still in the early stages when, on a morning that smelled like lightning and damp earth, I received a call from my friend Greeny, whom I had known since nursery school. He reported that a massive branch had fallen and smashed through my canoe, which was resting on sawhorses behind his house in Minneapolis.

I exhaled in a vaguely accusatory way. "Now what the hell am I going to paddle to Hudson Bay?"

I sped across the Lake Street bridge to his house on the other side of the Mississippi. The canoe, a 17-foot Royalex hull with ash seats, thwarts, and gunwales, had been with me since my sister Hawk gave it to me more than a decade earlier, when she moved to Colorado.

Growing up, Hawk was my idol. As a boy I shared a

bedroom with my younger brother, Adam, but I preferred to sleep in Hawk's room, on the floor beside her bed.

When I was 11 and Hawk was 13, she registered for a two-week session at a YMCA canoeing camp on West Bearskin Lake, along the Minnesota-Ontario border. I tagged along.

In subsequent years we camped with groups of kids our own age, but that first summer we went into the woods together. Sitting on a piney point on West Bearskin Lake, Hawk taught me how to smoke cigarettes and weed. She shared secrets that boys my age weren't supposed to know, and showed me menstrual blood as it traveled down her leg following a midnight swim. Out on trail in the Boundary Waters Canoe Area Wilderness, she was always much tougher than me. She paddled harder and complained less about grueling portages, hunger, mosquitoes, and wet sleeping bags. I had always looked up to her, and the canoe she gave me had special meaning.

Greeny and I used handsaws to extricate the mangled boat from the leafy fist that had impaled it through the stern. When we yanked the offending branches from the hull, the gashes, two jagged wounds the size of apples, appeared to be terminal. Nearly certain that Hawk's canoe would never float again, we gently loaded it onto my car.

I drove along River Road to downtown Saint Paul, and parked next to an unmarked loading dock behind an old brick warehouse. I climbed up a crumbling concrete lip and pounded on the garage door. Behind it I heard the proprietor of this underground repair shop bark impatiently, "Coming!"

Old Hal maintained no particular schedule, so I was thankful to find him at work. He opened the door and glared at me as if he were looking into the sun. The previous summer he had replaced the rotted gunwales on Hawk's canoe, so I knew this was just his gruff way.

I wandered around the shop while Hal examined the canoe. There were three wood-strip canoes on the floor in various stages of completion. These were Hal's projects, and they would eventually join the curvaceous masterpieces hanging on ropes from the ceiling. I couldn't help but wonder if Hal was grouchy because his love of canoes and skill in building and repairing them had led to his imprisonment in a dusty warehouse just two blocks off the Mississippi River, which he rarely got to paddle.

I looked at a grainy color photograph on the wall. It was an image of a covered one-man canoe rigged with a sail, beached on the sandy shoreline of a large lake surrounded by pine trees.

"I designed that boat," Hal offered half-heartedly. He went on to explain that the guy it belonged to had passed through Saint Paul recently. He was paddling from Patagonia to Alaska in stages.

"He came to me and asked for a canoe he could sail on

the big waters up North," Hal continued. "The guy takes winters off, but apart from those breaks he has been paddling constantly for four or five years."

This seemed like a real achievement to me, but Hal quickly discredited the effort. "He's a rich man and his kids are out of the house. He isn't married. No pets. No one to take care of but himself. What the hell else does he have to do?"

I thought about what I had to do. I took care of my three daughters and my son four days and three nights a week. I was constantly struggling with my ex-wife for custody of the kids. I had to figure out what I was going to do now that my three-year graduate program at the University of Minnesota was nearing completion. And I had to get a job in order to begin to repay my $30,000 student loan.

"Once I'm finished with it, this canoe will take you anywhere you want to go," Hal said.

"Even Hudson Bay?" I replied.

Hal's eyes softened. He invited me back to his office, set down a blue plastic barrel of the sort used in Minnesota to distribute salt on the roads, and ordered me to sit. He described how he had paddled many venerable waterways, including Great Slave Lake, the Yukon River, and the Border Route from Lake Superior to Lake of the Woods. The Sevareid route had always loomed above all others in his imagination, but he was getting too old to even think about it now. He offered me a grimy can of Diet Coke from the shelf above his computer.

"You'll need a shotgun: double-barreled, 20-gauge minimum, pump action. Anything smaller will just piss off the bears," he said. "The Canadians are insane about guns. They'll make you fill out a pile of paperwork before they let you bring one into their country—and even then they'll probably deny you entry."

Hal interrupted himself, logging onto the Web site for the Canada Firearms Centre and printing out a one-page declaration form, along with two pages of instructions.

"And when that polar bear attacks," Hal continued, as if it were inevitable, "you're going to have to unload on him. Pump and unload, right in the skull."

I couldn't help but smile. I had never seen Hal emote, but the thought of fighting off a polar bear had him really worked up.

"I don't care if that goddamn bear looks like a rug," he went on. "You just reload and empty, again and again. You can't be too careful. It's your life or his."

Hal calmed down slowly, then conceded that there "might not be bear issues," but only if proper care was taken.

I described my strategy for keeping predators out of camp. "I always string my food pack out of reach, between two trees."

"Suicide," he cried out in response, shaking his bald skull and wagging a finger. "You can't hang your food in the subarctic. The few trees on the tundra aren't tall enough to hang food out of reach of a polar bear. You lose your food supply, you starve. You need to carry your food in one of these things."

Hal pointed at the salt barrel I was seated on. Its thick plastic shell and metal locking ring would keep my food safe. He explained how a friend of his at the Department of Transportation had donated the barrels. Hal turned around and sold them to canoeists. He normally cleaned them up and charged $50 each, but he was offering to sell me two for that price, so long as I was willing to wash them myself.

When he was finished repairing Hawk's canoe, Hal proclaimed nonchalantly, it would be more durable than it was before the accident. Just in case, however, and in light of the fact that there were plenty of treacherous rapids and nasty waterfalls up on the Hayes River—the leg of the Sevareid route running some 500 miles northwest from Lake Winnipeg—he offered to sell me a patch kit that could be deployed easily in the backcountry.

"It may not look pretty," he explained, "but this stuff will firm up hard as nails over any puncture." I promptly paid for the kit, and agreed to return for the salt barrels and Hawk's canoe.

Ten days passed before Hal called to say that the canoe was "ready to paddle to the end of the Earth." It was a time of intense negotiation. After battling my ex-wife for 50 percent custody, I was asking our kids to stay with their mother for at least a dozen weeks while I inched up the globe in a canoe, a notion that prompted considerable indignation. Our two youngest kids, 6-year-old Malcolm and 13-year-old Martha, protested with particular vehemence. Only Gemma, our second child, encouraged me to go.

I concocted a ridiculous itinerary in an effort to satisfy everyone. I would shove off from the confluence of the Minnesota and Mississippi Rivers on April 15, return to Saint Paul from southwestern Minnesota two weeks later for Gemma's high school graduation, resume paddling for three weeks, and return home from the Canadian border for Martha's 14th birthday. Then I would go back to the river for three weeks, return home from northern Manitoba for Malcolm's 7th birthday, put in four more weeks on the river, and return home again on August 6, for Allison's 18th birthday. Finally, I would return to northern Manitoba for the last weeks of the trip, which I hoped to finish before Malcolm's first day of school, just after Labor Day.

When I described this plan to my old friend Kocher, hoping to find validation, he raised his eyebrows. "I don't think you should leave from Minneapolis. José isn't going to tolerate paddling upstream on the Minnesota River for three weeks. It will take you five days just to make Mankato, which is only an hour's drive from here. What's to stop him from calling one of his homies at that point and arranging for a pickup."

I was irritated by this insight, but I also knew that Kocher was right. He and I had been on enough expeditions to understand the screaming agony long-distance canoeing produces in the mind and body, and the overwhelming impulse to quit. I had to get far enough away so that José wouldn't have a lot of choices when he inevitably realized that paddling 35 to 40 miles a day was truly torturous.

Back at Midwest Canoe, Hal cleared paperwork from his desk and scribbled out my invoice. Then—after I had explained the situation with José, my insane itinerary, and my inability to come to terms with a starting point for the expedition—he set me straight. "You're not Sevareid," he spat. "You're not some teenage kid with nothing else to do. Who are you anyway?"

When I told him I was a graduate student at the University of Minnesota, Hal unleashed a tirade on the state of modern literature. It was "self-indulgent," he complained, and only reflected "the failure of our society to create original thinkers." I was astonished that this grumpy man who built and repaired canoes was so passionate about literature.

Hal went on to explain that paddling the nearly 500-mile stretch from Lake Winnipeg to the sea on the Hayes River was "like climbing Mount Everest, except that far more people summit Everest every year than reach Hudson Bay on the Hayes. It's the crown jewel of the canoeing world. The rest of Sevareid's route, the 1500 miles leading to the Hayes, is really just a driveway to the north end of Lake Winnipeg."

I confessed to Hal that I was unsure what the trip would accomplish if we didn't start in Minneapolis and end at Hudson Bay, as Sevareid had done.

This was the most preposterous thing he had ever heard. "Why would you want to do what someone else has done? Totally unoriginal. Are you Eric Arnold Sevareid? For Christ's sake, didn't you say you were a writer? Take this Indian–Puerto Rican kid, this José, and make the journey your own. *Canoeing with the Cree* has already been written. Write your own story. Write *Canoeing with José!*"

Over the following days, I checked out nearly 20 topographical maps covering Sevareid's entire route from an obscure campus library for geography majors. I took them home and pored over the charts, which were covered by blue veins of water and the green flesh of mother earth.

And then one afternoon, I dropped in to see José at Pawn Minnesota, as I had done almost every day since he agreed to come on the trip. Dressed in his freshly pressed uniform, a white shirt with narrow black tie, he bought and sold just about everything: hand tools, DVDs, video games, guitars, televisions, stereos, computers, MP3 players. My repeated visits provided opportunities to remind him about our impending departure, and to implore him to get a pair of glasses for the trip.

Nearly blind, José never noticed me until I was next in line at his counter.

"Good afternoon, sir," José said professionally.

"Did you get the stuff yet?" I whispered confidentially. I had given him a list of items to acquire before the day planned for our departure.

Each time I asked he seemed surprised, and each time

his reply was the same: "No, dawg, not yet. But I will." It was unnerving to be putting so much energy into researching the route and acquiring gear, unsure if José was serious about going.

When I unrolled the maps for him later that night at my apartment, José seemed uninterested. He looked away and changed the subject. His older brother had been released from prison recently after having raped an adolescent cousin, and he and José had met two young women, wealthy members of one of Minnesota's casino-rich Dakota tribes. They had moved in with these women, using them for their Escalades, condos, and booze. It was a cushy setup, and I feared José might never leave.

I pointed to the region north of Lake Winnipeg, where we would encounter treacherous white water and long stretches of wilderness. I also explained how we would have to be particularly mindful of polar bears.

"Oh, hell no, bro," he cried, "I ain't going into no polar bear territory. That ain't even close to how I'm going out. You for reals?"

I assured him I was, and went to the computer to search polar bears. The first listing was a polar bear fact sheet. Up came a colorful page from *Ranger Rick* magazine, illustrated with endangered species from around the world: a mountain gorilla bared his teeth and pounded his chest, a komodo dragon swiped the air with its razor-sharp claw, and a massive polar bear stalked a field of snow and ice.

José leaped back from the screen and backed away to the far side of the living room, shouting, "Hell no. Hell no. I ain't canoeing through no jungle with dragons and gorillas. Oh, fuck no. Are you insane, dawg? I ain't going."

I laughed aloud at the notion that these equatorial creatures would haunt our northern journey, then promised that there would be no gorillas or dragons, and that, in the unlikely event we were attacked by a polar bear, I would fill said predator with all the lead at my disposal. José seemed appeased for the most part, and we agreed again on the date of our departure, just a few days away.

Finally, the day before we were to set out, I left José in a van idling outside my ex-wife's building in downtown Saint Paul and climbed the five flights to her apartment. The ink was still fresh on our divorce, and I dreaded every interaction with Jane. I was 20 and she 24 when we first met in a Native American studies class at the University of Minnesota. She was pretty and outgoing, I was lonely and increasingly estranged from my family. And I couldn't help but fall in love with Jane's two-year-old daughter, Allison. In that brief initial period of purity in our relationship, I committed to raising Allison, and it was this that had kept us together through a series of moves across Minnesota, Spain, South Dakota, Texas, and Alaska.

We had shared incredible intimacy in our marriage, but in recent years Jane and I had come to distrust each other. And now I resented her for hovering as I hugged the kids and said a silent prayer. Having long subdued my emotions in her presence, I said goodbye without shedding any tears. But I couldn't help but linger at the door as Malcolm and Martha pleaded with their eyes for me to stay.

Kocher had agreed to help us get underway, paddling along for the first few days. And so it was that I found myself loading three Duluth packs and a food barrel into his Volkswagen van, and securing Hawk's canoe on top of the vehicle.

We stood on the sidewalk in front of my apartment, debating whether José would show. Two hours had passed since the departure time we'd agreed on, and José wasn't answering his phone.

Another hour passed before he picked up.

"Oh, we're leaving already? My man!" he said with faux surprise. "I'll be over in a minute. Gotsta have music, dawg."

I had warned him about taking electronic devices. They would be waterlogged at some point, I explained. And besides, I added, "You won't need music. The wind and the water make their own." Though I knew how lame it would sound to José, I meant this.

Another hour later, José rolled up in the passenger seat of a black Escalade. His new roommate, Homegirl J, was behind the wheel. He slid down to the street holding a shopping bag from Wal-Mart. He had on the white tank top and blue polyester shorts he would wear for the rest of the summer.

I had given José a list of essentials for the trip—wool socks, rain gear, hiking boots, a sweater, and a winter hat— items that would easily fill out a watermelon-sized sack. But there was just a little plastic bag hanging limply from his fist.

"You got enough gear in there to last you two months, bro?" I chided.

I opened the sack and found two pairs of boxer shorts still in their packaging, along with two tank tops, three pairs of white cotton socks, and a cotton sweatshirt. On a canoe trip to the subarctic, this was a just-add-water recipe for hypothermia. And it looked as if the kid still didn't have glasses.

"I did get these though," José said, grabbing the pair of oversized orange sunglasses that had been dangling from the neck of his T-shirt and sliding them onto his nose. "My stunner shades, bro. Gotsta have the stunner shades."

José noticed my frustration. "Nah, I'm foolin' with you, bro. We just need to pick up my new glasses at America's Best."

My spirits lifted. We could get whatever else he needed on our way to the Red River headwaters.

José's brother emerged from the back seat of the Escalade and circled the scene. José hadn't let him in on our plan. All D knew was that we were "going fishing in Canada for a few days." That bit of knowledge, combined with the fact that he had recently watched *Brokeback Mountain*, had D thinking, as José would later put it, "that we were up to some real homo shit."

D was a scary character, but I wasn't scared. Nor was I fearful of any element of the trip. Not the deep wilderness navigation nor the murderous whitewater, not the risky lake crossings nor the polar bears, nor the possibility of medical emergencies and starvation. I wanted to be swallowed by the wide green landscape, to escape my suffocating sadness and despair.

Apart from singing along with rap lyrics, José didn't say a word for a couple hours after we left Saint Paul. He lounged on the back bench of Kocher's van, hidden behind two pairs of glasses—the new eyeglasses from America's Best, covered by the stunner shades—moving and grooving to the thump of his headphones.

I wasn't surprised to see José acting hard around Kocher. Nor was I surprised that meeting José for the first time caused Kocher to question my sanity. He turned slightly to me with each of José's off-key eruptions, his expression at once amused and concerned.

I gazed out the window, taking in the yellow prairie of the western lakes region. I couldn't help but think with some regret about missing out on the Minnesota River, which paralleled our course some 50 miles south, beyond the rolling horizon.

When searching for a meaningful starting point, I had

placed a phone call to Kevin Jensvold, the chairman of the Upper Sioux Community, whose tiny reservation sits along the Minnesota River, some 250 miles upstream from Saint Paul. I asked if he'd be willing to meet with José before our departure from Upper Sioux. I knew how much it would mean to José to have a tribal chairman pat him on the back as he boarded a canoe for the first time. Recognition and acceptance from men in the Native community was particularly important to him.

Unfortunately, Jensvold informed me dismissively that he might be busy the day we planned to shove off. "If he needs encouragement, tell him I've heard stories of men who came through here before in canoes."

I asked Jensvold if there was anyone on his rez, a spiritual leader perhaps, who might be willing to come out to the river and speak with José. Jensvold said he would look into it and promised to call back. He never did.

I turned to the back of the van and shouted to get José's attention. I told him about the conversation I'd had with the Upper Sioux chairman and his apparent lack of interest in our undertaking. José said that kind of treatment was what he had come to expect from Native people, even members of his immediate family.

"That's how it goes, bro. Indians hear my name and think I'm just another Mexican. They don't give a shit."

José had told me before about how his brothers and sisters, of a Lakota mother and fathers of diverse nationalities (Somali, Ethiopian, Puerto Rican, Yemeni), had all experienced similar disdain from the greater Native community, who often derided them as illegitimate Indians. At Heart of the Earth, the Native charter school in Minneapolis where José had gone to high school, he was constantly getting into fights—particularly with the Anishinaabe boys—over the question of his Indian-ness. They hated him for being light skinned and having a Hispanic name, and he hated them for being Anishinaabe. He had been burned in romantic and business relationships with Anishinaabe people, and he clung to the historic animosity that lingered in Minnesota.

We pulled off the interstate in Alexandria, intending to eat lunch and round out José's paltry collection of gear at one of the discount stores along the strip. While searching for a restaurant we drove past the 30-foot statue of Big Ole, "the country's biggest Viking," outside the Runestone Museum. Home to the Kensington Runestone—a purportedly ancient tablet covered with writing said to be inscribed by pre-Columbian Viking explorers in 1362, and discovered by a local farmer in 1898—the site had since become a destination of sorts. The inscription on the stone reads as follows:

Eight Goths and 22 Norwegians on a journey of exploration from Vinland very far west. We had camp by 2 rocky islands one day's journey north from this stone. We were out fishing one day. After we came home we found 10 men red with blood and dead. AVM [Ave Maria] save from evil.

If the tablet is authentic, the Nordic travelers who inscribed it almost certainly came down from Hudson Bay, making the Runestone the earliest evidence of paddlers from the north Atlantic reaching Minnesota. Scientists and archaeologists had questioned its legitimacy for more than a century, but there was no debate as far as José was concerned. He had once participated in a discussion of the Runestone in a history class at Heart of the Earth, and his mind was made up.

"That rune thing is fugazi," he said, sneering at Big Ole's winged helmet. "To claim Norwegians were here 700 years ago sounds like a wild allegation to me." Instead, he speculated, the Runestone was inscribed by white men scheming to claim Minnesota from the Natives, an assertion that almost seemed to be confirmed by Big Ole. From behind a blond beard he gazed into the distance, as if beholding his conquest. The inscription on his shield read: "Alexandria, birthplace of America." As we pulled away, José saluted him with middle fingers out the rear window.

From Big Ole and the Runestone Museum we headed to Target, where I quickly lost track of José. I searched the men's clothing department, where I hoped he would be considering some warm clothes. Then Kocher and I searched for him in Health and Beauty, where we figured he'd be looking for toiletries like toothpaste, a toothbrush, and soap. We eventually found him in Music and Electronics, clutching a portable CD player, a grip of AA batteries, and discs by Mariah Carey and Young Jeezy.

Had I known that José was about to spend nearly all the money he had on entertainment, I would have blown a gasket. He'd told me he was planning to set aside two paychecks for the trip. But I would soon learn that he'd "loaned" most of that money to D and his grandmother, and left Saint Paul with about $50 in his pocket.

As we followed José back in the general direction of the registers, Kocher sensed my aggravation. "Don't worry about it," he whispered. "He'll figure it out once he's on the river." And on one level, Kocher was right. José had always lived with nothing, and he was well adapted to it. Kocher had kindly packed rain gear and a fleece sweater for him in any case, and I had a sleeping bag and pad.

From Alexandria we drove to Fargo and met up with my old friends Greeny and Huck, who had followed us to North Dakota in order to help with logistics and see us off. We parked Kocher's van in a ramp at a mall and piled into Huck's 4Runner for the 60-mile drive south to the headwaters. We planned to return to the van in three days, after paddling 100 river miles, at which point Kocher would drive home.

Greeny and Huck had been in my life for decades. As kids we banded together closely, boys seeking relief for varying reasons from our families of origin. It was with Greeny and Huck that I took my first bike trip, 250 miles from Minneapolis to the Wisconsin Dells, when I was just 14 years old. When I was 18, we took our first extended road trip, from Minneapolis to Key West, and from there to Montreal. After our freshman year in college, we met under the Arc de Triomphe in Paris, and spent the summer tramping across Europe, Scandinavia, and the British Isles. In subsequent years we pursued riskier adventures: traveling up the Amazon River, mountain climbing in Alaska, and hiking across Bolivia and Peru. Now Greeny and Huck both had young families and demanding professional lives.

Around midnight that night outside Wahpeton, the sky opened. We struggled to see through the foggy windshield, but eventually we found a dirt road leading in the direction of the Red River. I'd considered the trip for weeks, but many loose ends remained. I needed a dry place to sort through the gear and camping supplies. I'd intended to make my final choices at the point of departure, and as a result, none of the gear had been placed in waterproof containers.

Risking ridicule, I suggested we spend the night in a hotel, so I could get my shit together in a dry place. Huck and Greeny stared at me, unamused. "You want to spend the whole summer outside," they asked, "but you're afraid of a little rain?" I quickly conceded, and we agreed to camp along the river.

The following morning, as rain continued to fall in sheets, we were awakened by the electric-motor hum of a maintenance vehicle. Driving it was a worker in green coveralls, who pretended not to notice that our tents were set up between a sand trap and the 13th green, in the middle of a golf course.

I stuffed everything I could into our packs with indiscriminate haste, and then we drove into Wahpeton and ate a greasy breakfast at Fryn' Pan Family Restaurant, which was crowded that Sunday morning with starched churchgoers. They regarded us with glares of provincial intolerance as I worried about José. He looked nervous, exhausted, and uncharacteristically reserved. I tried to goad him out of his shell. "Hey bro, what's wrong with these people? They're acting like they've never seen an Indian before."

He took the bait. "I see it all the time, dawg. They're just worried papi gonna steal their wives." A roar of laughter rose from our table and I saw José smile for the first time in two days.

It was still raining when we found Headwaters Park & Boat Landing in Breckenridge, the town opposite Wahpeton on the Minnesota side of the river. It is here that the Bois de Sioux and Otter Tail Rivers flow into a small reedy lagoon before gathering in a single stream a few canoe lengths wide, forming the Red River of the North.

Seeing this spot for the first time flashed me back to "Red River Mud," the fifth chapter of *Canoeing with the Cree*. During their 21-day paddle up the Minnesota River, Sevareid and Port had met some farmers, killed a turtle for soup, and mucked around for a few frustrating days in the wetlands between the Minnesota and Bois de Sioux Rivers, before reaching this lagoon.

Kocher, José, and I posed for photographs with a four-sided granite pillar, which resembled the obelisks we would see later in towns along the Red River Valley, commemorating historic floods. This monument marked the start of the waterway, and an engraved map on it showed our route as far as Lake Winnipeg. After so many months of emotional uncertainty, the clarity was comforting.

We loaded our pregnant packs into the space between the thwarts, along with a food barrel, fishing poles, and a map tube as long as my arm. When Kocher stepped in, the canoe was precariously top-heavy.

José's first attempt to step into the bow of the canoe was aborted after he lost both unlaced boots in the mud lining the lagoon. He hauled them out with a slurp, put them back on his feet, and entered the boat hauling an additional five pounds of muck. When I pushed off into the weak current and slid gingerly into the stern, Hawk's canoe floated just a few inches above the murky waterline.

I thought of the opening line of *Canoeing with the Cree*: "We were off!"

But then we turned back not a hundred yards from the boat landing. José had left his glasses in the truck. Or so he thought, before discovering that they were in the pocket of his rain jacket.

Finally, we were off!

BROKEBACK BAPTISM

Thirty minutes into our voyage, I made a shoddy command decision. As we approached the whitewater created by a low-head dam, I mockingly paraphrased the campy training video I'd seen at a program in junior high. Kocher had attended the same program, and now he joined me in imitating the narrator:

The river's most perilous obstruction, the low-head dam, is a wall-like structure just below the surface. As water flows over it and drops, a backwash is created, trapping anything that floats. Even small low-head dams can become brutal death traps when river levels are high.

In this case the river surely was high, and the low-head was producing a class II rapid, with standing waves the size of sports cars.

I knew enough to avoid it, but Kocher encouraged us to run the dam. "This is way smaller than anything you'll see on the Hayes," he said. "You need the practice."

Due in equal parts to Kocher's ill-conceived encouragement

and to laziness, I decided to run the rapid rather than portage our overloaded canoe. Kocher grabbed the food barrel and a pack, and stood on land taking photos as we paddled back from the dam.

José twisted and winced. "We really gonna do this, dawg?"

I hadn't run a rapid of any consequence since I was 16 years old, paddling the Ogoki River in northern Ontario. All I had for José was baseless bravado. "We'll get through it," I said, "just paddle."

As we passed over the dam and swooshed down the rushing slide behind it, the canoe smashed into the first frothing line of standing waves. José was thrown onto one knee, and he grabbed the left gunwale with both hands. The canoe dipped left, the standing wave crashed over the rails, and river water filled the boat. José and I were pulled into the churning backwash along with our food and gear, then jettisoned unscathed from the lethal mayhem below the dam. As I popped to the surface, I found José clutching the partially submerged bow, his eyes wild with panic.

"Stay with the canoe, and keep your feet out in front of you," I shouted. "You're alright! Your life jacket will float you."

We swam the canoe to shore and began corralling our tackle box, the GPS receiver, and whatever else we could find. As we were doing so, I looked upstream and saw Kocher in trouble.

He was standing in the current below the dam, up to his chest in roiling pandemonium, weighted down by the

80-pound Duluth pack strapped to his back. Demonstrating fearlessness and the superhuman strength I had come to expect from him, Kocher trudged to land, then continued over to where we were standing waist-deep against the steep rocky bank, emptied his hands of supplies, and fished us out of the river with an outstretched hand.

I was eager to empty the boat and get back in the water, but José was furious. "Why the fuck did you do that? You tipped us. You said we'd get through it."

I ignored him, focused on emptying and then reloading the canoe. As we returned to the river, I noticed a bearded man in a black pickup parked across the channel near the dam. I had seen the same vehicle at the boat landing in Breckenridge. The driver was watching us, smiling cruelly.

I could see the rage in José's eyes. As if things weren't bad enough, now a redneck was laughing at him. Standing knee-deep in the water, he demanded to use my phone. He said he was going to call Homegirl J, so she could come pick him up. I dug the soaked phone out of a dripping pack and handed it to him. José burrowed into the duffer spot, pulled his headphones over his ears, and went unresponsive.

Kocher and I paddled a docile draw over the next mostly sunny 25 miles. Around every bend, as if the river hadn't seen humans since Sevareid, deer bolted between the cottonwoods, and bald eagles, startled from their nests, took wing on fabulous spans, often swooping down to take a closer look at us. Canadian geese honked, warning us to keep our distance, and scurried to shore to shepherd goslings among the vegetation. Throughout this first extended leg of the voyage, José spit out C-Murder lyrics, moving only to slap with his paddle at the larger geese when they swam close to the boat.

I'd taken some difficult kids out on the water, but I'd never seen anyone show such disdain for Mother Earth. Kocher didn't have to turn around to see my frustration. Per usual, though, his analysis was sage. "He's creating his own little urban environment inside those headphones," he explained. "It's going to take time. You have to be patient."

We stopped for the night at a city park in Abercrombie, North Dakota. There wasn't much to the place beyond grass, an outhouse, a dock, and a lighted gazebo.

The rain returned, but we stayed dry under the gazebo while Kocher prepared a deluxe dinner from ziplocked ingredients. We had pita sandwiches stuffed with thick cuts of mozzarella, sweet heirloom tomatoes, spinach, arugula, fresh-squeezed lemon juice, and mint.

José fished from shore on his own, ignoring my request that he wait to wet his line until we had a fishing license, and disregarding appeals to help set up the tent or assist in preparing the meal. I was increasingly frustrated. When it came to expeditions, I knew only one way to behave, and it was based on an unwritten code I had learned from the trip leaders who first took me into the wilderness:

- Don't dive into a river without first checking for submerged objects.

- Don't let canoes touch anything but air and water, lest they tear and make it impossible to paddle home.
- Don't reach into the communal trail mix bag with your hand, lest you spread intestinal disease to the rest of the group.
- Don't run in camp or on trails, lest you twist an ankle and burden the group with your evacuation.
- Always strap Duluth packs to thwarts to prevent them from sinking in the event of capsizing in deep water.
- Never wash dishes in a lake or stream; soap and food waste are environmentally invasive.
- Make sure camp is set and all chores complete before engaging in nonessential activities.

As a novice I had rebelled against these strictures, which seemed to take all the fun out of canoe trips. But over the years I had come to understand their utility.

The following morning, José stashed the fishing pole a minute before the sheriff arrived in camp on a black S-10. A middle-aged white man in Wranglers and a cowboy hat, he initially didn't identify himself, choosing instead to poke around our campsite, his six-year-old son in tow, asking about our intentions.

This would be the first of several encounters we had with law enforcement. Whether it was the fact that we were an unusual pair of travelers heading toward an international border in an age of terrorism hysteria or simply the kind of harassment people of color endure every day in America, our trip seemed to be viewed by government officials as a criminal act. In fact, we would be interrogated by officials from five different agencies by the time we crossed into Canada.

While their approaches varied, they all asked the same questions. How do you two know each other? Where are you going? How long do you expect the trip to take? How did you get time off for such a long trip? How will you know where you're going? What are you going to eat? Why are you doing this?

After seeing José lose his cool at the sight of these authority figures the first couple times we encountered them, each jittery utterance sketchier than the last, I invariably took the lead in handling the exhanges. My responses were cautious and truthful. I was José's mentor. We had met five years earlier at New Voices, a Minneapolis-based journalism program for Native American youth. We expected our trip on the Red, Nelson, Echimamish and Hayes Rivers to take roughly two months. José's employer had granted him a leave of absence for the summer. I was a teacher, so I had summers off. We were navigating with topographical maps, compasses, and a GPS receiver. For sustenance we had freeze-dried camping food.

Invariably, the officer would nod suspiciously in response, then run our names for warrants. But the trickiest part of these interrogations was inventing answers in response to that last question: Why are you doing this? The question always seemed to imply that no sane person would undertake such a journey without sinister motives. Here too, though, I went with a clipped version of the truth: the trip was about physical and spiritual renewal.

This last point almost always signaled closure to these absurd exchanges, greeted as it was by looks of utter astonishment. For as anyone who is even vaguely familiar with the Red River knows, it is one of the most unforgiving waterways in America. And yet, the torture entailed by canoeing 10 or 12 hours each day to cover 30 or 40 miles, eating and sleeping on riverbanks that were essentially mud pits, baking under the withering sun, and freezing through frequent cloudbursts was, for us both, a welcome respite from the heartache and stress that had come to dominate our lives in Saint Paul. Particularly in this first stage of the journey, our days on the river entailed a strong element of self-mutilation. The physical pain and demands of the travel relieved our suffering hearts.

Because there was no freshwater available at the city park and the river was too brown with sediment for our filtration equipment, we decided to walk into town to fill our jugs before shoving off. We climbed up the riverbank and found a narrow trail that led up a leafy incline. In the deep shade of the willows the air turned uncomfortably chilly. José and Kocher, walking before me, stopped simultaneously.

"Do you smell that?" Kocher asked.

José sniffed. "It smells like old blood."

Kocher agreed. "It's creepy in here."

I wasn't sure what I smelled—rusty iron, perhaps—but I felt claustrophobic and pushed forward to take the lead.

We emerged shortly thereafter on a sunny prairie, in the middle of which stood an old Army post consisting of a few hastily constructed cabins. This was Fort Abercrombie, founded in 1857 to protect the valley's early white settlers.

During the US-Dakota War of 1862, Dakota warriors repeatedly attacked the fort, sneaking up from their canoes on trails like the one we had just walked. Few Indians were able to penetrate the withering hail of gunfire, and according to historians, dozens had been killed in the effort to make their way through the dense willows between the river and the garrison. When I shared this with Kocher and José, we all agreed that this was hallowed ground.

We filled our jugs at the local pub, which appeared to be the only active establishment in town. It was a couple hours past sunrise, but already the stools were humming with what must have been a good portion of Abercrombie's population. The townies were welcoming, and the bartender topped us off with a genuine smile.

José remained in the doorway while Kocher and I went inside. I noticed him scanning the all-white locals with a worried expression. I thought his fear unwarranted in this case, but after the haunting walk from the river, he was in no mood to test their tolerance. When we came out a few minutes later, José was gone, making his way back to the river.

PARADISE LOST

We traveled the 77 river miles between Abercrombie and Fargo over two punishing days. A northerly headwind eliminated any advantage provided by the current, and we struggled to make headway. With temperatures hovering in the mid-forties and a near-constant downpour, my bared arms turned to frigid slabs. Kocher settled into the sloshing puddle at the center of the canoe, sacrificing his body to the chills that inevitably resulted from inactivity. In the bow, José cowered beneath a rain hood, muttering obscenities and dipping his paddle weakly.

After what felt like dozens of hours of relentless pummeling, we began scouting the grey riverbanks for a campsite. We were just 30 miles north of Abercrombie, and it was challenging to identify a spot that would support a tent on the swampy banks looming up steeply from the water.

Several miles beyond the point where our search for a campsite began, Kocher spotted a farm field atop a 30-foot precipice. "My ass cannot get any soggier," he explained, having soaked in the mire for at least 10 hours. "We're stopping here."

We struggled up the slippery pitch, hauling only the tent, sleeping bags, a water jug, and trail mix. We left the rest of the gear behind in the canoe, which was tied off for the night on a logjam

We pitched our tent on a truck-wide swath of un-cultivated soil, between a meadow planted with soybeans and the edge of the soggy promontory. We spread our sleeping bags, crawled inside the tent, and ate a quick dinner of trail mix and water. By sunset we were asleep, our muddy bodies filling the dome's dead air with un-pleasant aromas.

The following morning, we descended through the mud and tiptoed across floating tree trunks to the waiting canoe. Kocher came down the jam last, heaving a pack before him. He stood at the edge of the canoe, considering how to get into the boat. Then, in one hasty move, he manhandled the weighty pack and dropped his body, ass first, into the boat. The canoe's crew and contents would have been upset and submerged in thick, smelly muskeg had I not made a split decision to rebalance the load, splashing overboard into the stagnant pool. When I emerged, neck deep in the shit, I saw that José felt badly. "That's rough, bro," he said, sympa-thy in his voice.

I pulled myself up over the gunwales, silently relishing the opportunity to show José how tough I was. When I met Kocher's glare I recognized immediately that his flop had been motivated by the fact that this was the lousiest three-day adventure imaginable. José and I had weeks of paddling ahead of us, and at least a vague sense that this miserable beginning would be repaid with warm tailwinds, magnificent campsites, and redemption in the rapids. But this was as good as it would get for Kocher. This was the most time he had taken off in years, and he was spending it in the mud of the Red River Valley.

Thirty miles south of Fargo, the skies opened. Animated by the force of Kocher's awesome temper, we pounded through the showers for several hours.

As cold hard rain turned to drizzle, bloody effluent streamed down the banks, turning the river red. The air smelled of sour flesh, and we saw the grey walls of a meat processing plant rising in the distance. Armies of carnivorous flies descended, turning the white canoe black. José pulled his hands into his rain jacket, covered his head with a grimy T-shirt, and swatted his back and shoulders after each vicious bite, shouting repeatedly, "Jesus fucking fuck."

Finally we arrived, weary and humbled, at the docks of Fargo's Lindenwood Park and Campground. We had paddled 40 hard river miles that day, 100 altogether over the first three days of the trip, and we weren't going an inch farther. We paid their cursed camping fee and began unloading the canoe.

The gum-snapping teen at the campground's headquarters was incredulous when we told her what we had done. "That's not even possible. You can't paddle a canoe from Wahpeton to here. Even if you could, that's like 70 miles— it would take weeks."

The recognition that we had done something that was unheard of in these parts gave us no small sense of satisfaction.

"We ain't no little bitches," José said, puffing up with pride.

"Hell no we ain't," Kocher agreed, snickering conspiratorially.

We pitched our tent on a campsite beside a young couple with a baby. Their vintage VW van sparked Kocher's curiosity, and he walked over to strike up a conversation with them.

Kocher returned with the van's owner, a man named Noah Suby. Noah offered us a ride across town to retrieve Kocher's vehicle, and José volunteered to stay behind and watch the camp.

As we drove, searching for the parking ramp where we'd stashed Kocher's van, we swapped stories with Noah. He was crisscrossing the continent with his family, filing quirky human-interest stories for Radio Free Bisbee, a station in Bisbee, Arizona. He had been attracted to Fargo by the region's geology.

Growing up in the desert Southwest, Noah explained, he'd become interested in the Red River primarily because of its status as the only river in the country apart from the San Pedro (which runs within 15 miles of Bisbee) to flow north. As he talked, I was struck by how much more Noah knew about the natural history of the northern plains than we did. Noah told us about Lake Agassiz, and how the Red River was a remnant of an inland sea that covered parts of what are now Minnesota, North Dakota, Saskatchewan, Ontario, and Manitoba. Covering an area 700 miles long by 200 miles wide, Agassiz covered more surface area than the present-day Great Lakes combined. This was news to me and Kocher.

Noah asked if we remembered the flood that devastated Grand Forks, North Dakota, in 1997. I recalled images of frantic residents erecting sandbag dikes in the pouring rain, but Noah explained that officials had evacuated some 50,000 people from the valley that year. Apparently Grand Forks, which was located some 160 river miles north of Fargo, had been built on the bed of Lake Agassiz—land so flat, he said, "you can stand on your tiptoes and see a hundred miles." He went on to explain that many scientists now believe Lake Agassiz melted and drained due to a rapidly warming climate around 7000 BC, causing sea levels to rise around the world, and possibly touching off the Biblical flood.

We found Kocher's van, and Noah and I returned to Lindenwood Campground to find José where we'd left him, seated at the picnic table. I told José that Noah had decided to do a story about our journey for his radio station. Then I asked Noah to tell José about Lake Agassiz and the great flood that created this flat region.

"That's some shit," José replied. "People in Grand Forks is stupid if they built their shit on a lake, then act all surprised when they get wet."

Noah nodded, then took out his digital recorder and sat

down at our picnic table with José and me. Wary of the long arm of the law, José agreed to be interviewed only if Noah would call him Joe. It was a policy we maintained as we approached the border, where traveling as José would only increase the likelihood of trouble.

Noah later mailed me a CD of the conversation, and I was struck by how, with the recorder switched on, José mutated into "Joe," a reticent silhouette of his former self.

"This is Noah and I'm here on the banks of the Red River in Fargo, North Dakota, with Jon Lurie and Joe Perez, who are camping for the night before continuing their journey northward. These two gentlemen are paddling from the border between South and North Dakota to the Hudson Bay."

"Joe, how did you get involved in this trip?"

"Well, my friend here, Jon Lurie, just suggested it one day. When he asked what I was doing this summer, I had no idea. So he just laid it all out for me, and I agreed."

"I heard there was a little mishap on the first day. Do you want to tell us about that, Joe?"

"About an hour into the trip we tried to run a dam and went into the river. What else is there to say?"

The clouds dissolved as we talked with Noah, and for the first time since being sucked into the river we had a dry patch of earth on which to air out our dank gear. The books I'd brought—*A Field Guide to the Edible Plants of North America, Song of the Paddle: An Illustrated Guide to Wilderness Camping, Guide to Backcountry Survival Techniques, Wilderness Rivers of Manitoba, Canoeing with the Cree*—were all sopping bricks, as was my hardcover journal. I placed the volumes on a picnic table to dry, the first step in a process that would ultimately take a month.

Our electronics were in hopeless condition. My cell phone, iPod, and digital camera were dead, as was José's CD player. I was shocked to see José take the loss in stride.

"Ain't no thing," he said. "I can fix it."

Apparently he had picked up some tricks for reviving electronics at the pawn shop. Customers often came into the store trying to hock gadgets that had been waterlogged. José convinced many of them to leave their iPods and cell phones for "recycling." After applying "ghetto repair techniques," José would make a few bucks pawning the functional devices.

Sitting at the picnic table, José used my Leatherman to disassemble his CD player. When he finished prying apart the case, removing the screws, pulling out the circuit boards, and unplugging the candy-striped diodes, parts were scattered everywhere—on the bench, in his lap, and in the grass at his bare toes. I was certain this effort would be futile.

I was wrong.

After dabbing the electronic guts with the corner of a bandanna, José reached into his pack and produced an "all-purpose hood utility kit"—a pack of Kool Menthols. He was trying to quit smoking, but he had brought them along in case of emergency. He promptly lit up two cigarettes and dragged them down while holding the components close to his lips, saturating them in a stream of smoke.

"This is how you do it, bro. The smoke dries that shit out."

Less than an hour later, José swaggered around the campground, gesturing wildly with his hands and vocalizing at maximum volume, seemingly oblivious to the frightened families looking on.

Later that evening, after José had been passed out in the tent for several hours, Kocher and I sat in the back of his van, conversing in hushed tones. On the eve of his planned departure, I was trying in vain to think of an angle that would convince him to continue paddling with us.

Kocher could hear the turmoil raging in my brain. To avoid being confronted with it, he inventoried the food he had accumulated for us, some of which had been stored in the van for the past few days. "A half pound of gouda cheese," he reported in a monotone. "Three dozen garlic-flavored crostinis; two sacks of salted and shelled pistachios; three half-pound pouches of teriyaki beef jerky; one large sack of organic dried fruit; two packages of Fig Newmans."

This went on until the eastern skies glowed faintly amber, and culminated in one final exhausted exchange.

"Are you sure you're not coming?"

"I wish I could, brother."

By the time the sun rose over the prairie on the Minnesota side of the river I had organized everything into two piles. Gear that was already damaged (camera) or deemed superfluous (screen tent) was stacked to my left. Gear deemed vital (GPS unit, water purifiers, maps, clothing, food) was stacked to my right.

I passed out in the back seat of the van for a couple hours, then awoke to the sound of Kocher slamming open the van's side door, nearly scalping me. He yanked the Duluth packs past my face and onto the grass. "Time to get up," he commanded. "I gotta get home to the dogs, and I got a ton of work around the house before I go back to work." I could tell Kocher was feeling bad about leaving us, and perhaps a bit envious.

I managed to slow him down somewhat. We ate breakfast in Fargo, then drove to a sporting goods store to score a new rain jacket for me.

Upon returning to the campground, Kocher remained in the van. He refused to snap photos and declined to help carry gear to the river's edge. He didn't even wave farewell after we loaded the canoe. He simply drove off before we paddled away.

The canoe was strikingly lighter without Kocher, but it would take some time for us to get used to the new balance. José rode high in the bow, and had to reach to get his paddle in the water.

It took two hours to paddle five miles into a warm wet headwind. When we reached Fargo North Dam, we portaged around the low-head, stepping precariously across a field of white retaining stones that slipped like basketballs beneath our boots. José carried a pack and the paddles. I carried the canoe overhead, the yoke burrowing into my shoulders.

Some 200 yards downstream, I set the canoe down at the end of a frothing churn. And as I did so, I said hello to a Native man fishing with his two little boys, their bobbers swirling in the fizz.

When José heard the guy was Anishinaabe from the nearby White Earth Reservation, he shifted into high gear, eager to demonstrate what Lakota people can do. Leaping from rock to rock, José bounded past the dam, hefted the food barrel and equipment pack onto his shoulders, and started back on trembling knees. Watching him trip and twist under the burden, it was easy to imagine José popping a fibula. But he eventually disgorged his load in a heap beside the canoe, sniffed at the fisherman and his boys, and shrugged his shoulders dismissively.

The little boys, with matching buzz cuts, begged for a canoe ride. We told them it wasn't safe to paddle in the rapids without a life jacket. The man asked lots of questions, then said that what we were doing sounded "pretty cool."

Finally, we shoved off.

"They got Indians!" José whispered back over his shoulder. "I thought it was going to be all rednecks up here." I could hear the pride in his voice, and knew he thought he had impressed them.

"Hey," yelled the older boy from shore, "where are you going?"

José turned back to him and smiled. "Hudson Bay, my nigga!"

RED RIVER MUD

n *Canoeing with the Cree*, Eric Sevareid sums up the 160 river miles between Fargo and Grand Forks, North Dakota, in one blasé paragraph: "The journey down the Red River from Fargo had been almost uneventful, a long, monotonous process of steady paddling, with no current to aid us, around unending bends, under a hot sun, beside muddy banks."

Some things don't change. We had agreed to a daily goal of 40 river miles, but 15 miles out of Fargo, José was hungry and refusing to paddle unless he had a hot meal.

It was impossible to cook lunch, I explained. There were no dry landings, the stove was buried somewhere in the depths of our packs, and we would have to use precious drinking water. We also had plenty of food that required no preparation: trail mix, jerky, dried fruit, chocolate, cheese, and crackers.

"It ain't real food unless it's cooked," he replied. "I can't live on birdseed."

I was increasingly frustrated by José's rickety stroke, and eventually I agreed to search for a relatively hospitable bank. Ankle-deep in inky goop, I fired up the single-burner camp stove and let José have at it. He boiled oriental-flavored ramen and fried squares of summer sausage, then combined them to make soup. I swatted flies off my back, and watched the conveyor flow past without us.

After filling his belly with a hot meal, José paddled hard until sundown, by which point we had logged just 25 miles since setting out that morning. We had had enough for the day, but our map showed no campsites or landings nearby. I anxiously searched the shore for a bivouac in the dying light, but this part of the river wound through a vast grassy wetland. I couldn't find a circle of earth that would support a tent.

As the last solar strands were extinguished by the closing sky, the darkness became absolute. We pulled on our headlamps and scanned the shores, the beams lighting steam phantoms rising from the surface. An unsettling quiet moved in with the mist, and although we discussed possibly paddling all night, we were both exhausted, a little spooked, and anxious for our sleeping bags.

Suddenly a shot rang out, so close we could feel it in our bones.

José fell forward and thrust his chin between his knees.

Another blast, this one closer. José stayed low and looked back at me. "What the fuck, dawg? Rednecks is shooting at us? This is some *Deliverance* shit."

Just then I saw the ripple from a beaver's tail shiver against the side of our boat.

"I ain't getting raped out here," José continued obliviously, "tell you that right now."

Eventually a wet furry head swam across the beam from his headlamp, prompting José to climb back onto his seat and resume paddling.

After some time, we came to the County Road 26 bridge. The covered earth beneath it would have worked, but José wasn't having it. He said he would only camp in a "designated campsite—one on the map."

The Red River was a new canoe route for the Minnesota DNR, and they had only published one of three maps planned for this region. In 10 miles we would depart the area it covered, and the only promising designation between our location and the edge of the map was four to five miles downstream, at the junction of the Sheyenne River. Called "Catch Big Cats," it was marked with the key symbols for "outfitter" and "lodging."

José was convinced that this was where we should stay. "We'll get a room, have a shower, order up a pizza, some room service maybe."

I had a feeling this place would not be that kind of party. I read the description from the map aloud: "Catch Big Cats Guide Service. Private catfish guiding and lodging." Sounded to me like redneck central.

José was insistent. "It's on the map!"

We reached the Sheyenne River around 11:00 p.m. I stood up in the canoe and searched for a streetlamp or the outline of a bunkhouse. But the only distinguishing feature was the slender black ribbon of the Sheyenne, squiggling southwest.

In spite of the fact that I had monitored our progress all day, the GPS readings matching precisely the location of every landmark along the way, José accused me of not knowing how to read a map. I asked him to consider the possibility that the map was inaccurate. Or perhaps Catch Big Cats was far enough off the river that we had missed it. After all, the mud along these banks was far too soft to support a permanent structure. José sulked.

Two hours and 10 miles later, the air cooled considerably and it began to rain. Shivering, José agreed to camp anywhere.

Knee-deep in silt, we struggled to pitch the tent on a random bank. We threw our gear inside, abandoned our buried boots, and dove in for the night. I sat up for about an hour, writing in my journal and waiting for the crud on my legs to solidify so I could scrape it off. José slithered into his bag with no hesitation, his head on the tent's mushy floor.

The following day we were visited by enormous bald eagles—the most impressive sight I'd ever encountered in the wild. They flew out of cottonwoods overhanging the river, their massive wingspans thumping like helicopter rotors, close enough that the downdraft stirred the hair on my head.

Oblivious to the eagles, José rapped Kanye West and slapped his paddle at the geese, whose startled honking once again overwhelmed the sound emanating from his cheap headset. His disrespect for the sacred drama playing out on our flanks was irritating. It was increasingly difficult for me to control my temper, but I remembered Kocher's advice.

At one point an eagle feather floated off the bow and drifted past the canoe. I noticed too late to grab it.

"Back paddle!" I shouted.

José yanked his headphones off and leaned on his paddle. I reached for the feather and held it up for him to behold. He was stunned, his expression mirroring my own sense of astonishment. This was the first time either of us had found an eagle feather.

It felt like an otherworldly acknowledgment of our journey. As if this feather, long and slender, with a black and grey blade, a thick ivory quill, and a delicate downy plume at its base, had been meant for us. I handed it to José. He considered it silently, gently stroking its soft edges with the tips of his fingers.

We covered an additional 25 miles before an icy deluge assaulted my blistering sunburn with pins and needles. For a second night we scrambled to shore and camped on a random slice of slithering tar. José was grouchy with hunger, so I fired up the stove under the vestibule and helped him cook ramen. I made do with a handful of trail mix.

José's mood did not improve following his meal. In the darkness of our improvised campsite, he castigated me for not having purchased a gun yet. I was planning to buy one in Grand Forks, where, according to some research I had done before we set out, there would be a large sporting goods store near the river. I had decided that there was no point in carrying a heavy shotgun on a portion of the trip that was almost surely free of the kind of perils that might require firepower.

José was increasingly exasperated. "They could kill us out here," he whined, apparently referring to bears and wolves. Then he began amassing a barricade of gear between his body and the tent wall.

I challenged him. "I thought you said you were Lakota?"

"Damn right I'm Lakota!" he shot back, all smugness and rage.

"The Lakota men I know understand what it means to find an eagle feather. This is more powerful than a gun. This feather offers spiritual protection."

The three years I spent on the Rosebud Reservation in my early twenties had provided me with a deep appreciation for Lakota spirituality. I had spent hundreds of hours as a boy at Hebrew school, and been Bar Mitzvahed at the Western Wall in Jerusalem. But my experience with organized religion paled in comparison with the spiritual power I felt during my first five minutes in a sweat lodge ceremony.

José fell silent. He took the feather from my hand and held it by the quill, twisting it in the lantern's glow. He twice opened his mouth as if to speak, but swallowed the words.

José shook his head. "I can't believe a white guy played the Indian card on me."

He admitted I was correct, however, and agreed that the eagle feather was a potent spiritual message that should not be discounted or ignored. As he put it at the time, "This is some hella powerful shit, dawg."

The following day, we paddled 40 miles without the familiar theatrics. We made camp in the darkness and walked three miles into Climax, a town of just a few hundred souls, hoping to find something open for dinner. As we approached the outskirts, we heard the clichéd strains of "Sweet Home Alabama."

At the end of the road a darkened gas station stood beneath the cool glow of a streetlamp. As we neared it, we noticed red neon lights down one of the side streets. Suddenly, a teenage girl with white running shoes bounded out of another alley and jogged toward the crimson glow.

José tried to get her attention. "What up, girl?" he called, loud enough to wake the neighbors. "Come give some love to papi!"

She kicked toward an invisible finish line at the far end of town, where I imagined her breathlessly calling 911.

Considering the urgency with which he needed indoor plumbing, I was surprised José had even noticed her. He ran around the bend and disappeared into the Corner Bar, a crowded honky-tonk with a couple of pool tables, a jukebox blaring, and a lot of cowboys. I found a table near the door and scanned the menu.

After waiting for José for a good long time, I went ahead and ordered. The leathery woman who waited on me initially seemed sympathetic, but then she asked if I was with "that skinny tan guy in the life jacket."

"Yeah," I replied, "that's my partner." I could tell by the burn in her eyes that she thought José was my love slave.

"He's been in the bathroom for a very long time," she said. "What is he doing in there?"

"He probably has diarrhea." I smiled, hoping the straightforward response would back her up.

She examined my life jacket as if it were a suicide vest. "I hope he's OK," she said facetiously.

José and the food appeared around the same time. He pushed away the cheeseburger I'd ordered for him. "Oh, hell no, bro. I ain't eating no burger right now." He didn't need to explain.

I had cheese curds, grilled cheese, and cheese fries—the vegetarian plate, as it were. While I ate and José fought to catch his breath, a commotion rose up around the pool tables. A guy in a Monsanto cap, obviously drunk, shouted, "Fuck you! Why don't *you* get the hell out of here?" He and another dude in a John Deere cap starting cross-checking each other with pool cues.

The vibe in the bar turned uglier as a crowd gathered around the two men. I looked to the waitress as a barometer of concern. She was behind the bar, rubbing down bottles of Jack Daniels and Smirnoff with a dishcloth, unmoved by the pending conflagration.

She noticed me looking at her, then walked over to address the guys we would soon come to call Bo and Luke

Duke of Polk County. We couldn't hear what she said to them, but we heard the response.

"Come on, Mom, we're just fucking around."

My mother would have washed my mouth out with soap, but this lady remained calm. The fighting stopped and their conversation continued; it was quickly apparent that they were talking about us. In unison, half the patrons in the crowded bar turned and glowered at José and me.

It was obviously time to hightail it back to the river, but as we moved to leave, the Dukes approached our table.

"Hey," said Bo, a slim 25-year-old in filthy Wranglers with stringy blond hair falling from the brim of his cap to his shoulders. "Leaving already? You ain't even touched your food."

Bo and Luke slid into our booth. "Hey, you boys ain't from around here. Let us buy you a drink," said Luke, a little too friendly. "What'll ya have?"

José looked to me for guidance. I didn't see any alternative but to engage them.

I asked for what I thought would be a typical order in this joint. "How about a Budweiser?"

"Well, ain't you fancy," sneered Bo. "You must be one of them city boys down from Grand Forks." He turned to José. "What are you?"

"Nah, I'm good," replied José.

I stepped in. "He's only 19."

"My brother didn't ask what he wanted to drink," explained Luke. "He asked what you are, Mexican or what?"

"Oh, hell no," offered José with innocent pride. "I ain't no fucking Mexican."

I was puzzled by the way they had identified José as Mexican. After all, Climax wasn't exactly old El Paso.

Then Bo broke the tense pause, shouting over Garth Brooks's "Friends in Low Places." "Hey, Mom, three Budweisers!"

As we tipped our fancy lagers the Dukes subjected us to a thorough inquest. It soon became clear that they had suspected us of being cops. There'd been "some troubles," and "certain busybodies who should mind their own fucking business" were pointing fingers at them. We told them about our trip. They listened, their eyes glassy.

At some point they seemed to be so captivated by the narrative that they forgot to distrust us. "Whoa," exclaimed Bo, "I ain't never heard of nobody covering all those miles on the Red, not even in a fishing boat!"

They stood and gathered their balance. "You guys have to come party with us," said Luke, the words painfully slurred. "We're going to every bar in Polk County—Crookston, East Grand Fork, Nielsville—we're going to tear it the fuck up. Come on, there's some ladies waiting for us in Crookston. You guys like pussy, don't you?"

José looked at me.

I shook my head.

"Pussy, bro," he whispered with the desperation of a teenage boy.

"No chance," I replied, quietly but emphatically.

They moved for the door. Bo had the keys to his General Lee twirling round his index finger. I felt a responsibility to ask if he was good to drive.

"We do this every weekend," said Luke. "Ain't no cops around here. This town's only cop ain't even real. He's a rent-a-cop, a security guard. That little bastard wouldn't dare pull us over."

We walked out ahead of the Dukes and found ourselves face to face with the little bastard, sitting in his squad car at the curb. The Dukes disappeared as he demanded our IDs.

"We had a report of two men with backpacks," said the rent-a-cop, a small white man with a scraggly moustache.

For the third time since entering this sticky little back-water, we were compelled to explain our presence.

"It's not illegal to carry backpacks, is it?" I asked.

"No," he said unapologetically. "I'm just responding to the complaint. There's no reason to get belligerent. What brings you two to Climax?"

"We're canoeists," José explained.

Eager to wrap up this encounter with the talking moustache in the Crown Victoria, I moved between the squad car and José and answered the remaining questions: "Are you on the run from the law? Do you two have any outstanding warrants? What will I find when I run your names?"

Suddenly the grilling was interrupted by the deafening

squeal of the Dukes' beat-up Charger roaring by on Main Street. Sure that the officer would go after them, I watched their smoking tires with relief.

Unmoved by the flagrant challenge, he finally asked where we were camped. When I told him we were under the bridge by the river, he flipped on his cherries and tore away in the direction of our camp.

We walked after him into the darkness, surrounded by the clicking and buzzing of katydids from the meadows, and then watched with dread as the red and blue strobes dipped beneath the dark horizon.

"Why did you tell him where we camped?" José scolded. "You need to learn how to keep your damn mouth shut."

He was right. "Lesson learned," I said.

Back at camp we found our belongings untouched. In the light of our headlamps, we tracked the officer's footprints from where they began at the edge of the road to where they turned back after thrashing about in the knee-deep mud.

"Them assholes were right," José proclaimed. "That little cop is a bitch."

THE EAGLE SPEAKS

Several hours past Halstad, a virtual ghost town of 600 people we passed on the fifth day of our journey, José decided he was in too much pain to continue, and went on strike again. He stowed his paddle and reclined on the packs, groaning, "Hell no, bro, my shoulder."

I pretended not to hear him. I knew well the distress José was experiencing. It was real and it was brutal. It had been four days since my head enjoyed a full range of motion; electric shocks blasted down my neck to my hands with every stroke. But this was what I had expected when setting out. This was how I had always experienced canoe trips—pleasure only ever followed torture. José, on the other hand, had no idea how much it was going to hurt.

I took swift action, digging the stove and a pan out of a pack. Processed foods were José's medicine on the river, and I would learn to use them like carrots.

José whistled Cam'ron as he fired up the burner and emptied a can of Beefaroni into a pan as we glided along on a meek current. I paddled while he cooked and ate dinner in the bow, making three miles by the time he lit his post-meal cigarette.

José paddled into the evening to the steady rhythm bumping out his headphones. I was glad for the resumed effort, but increasingly lonely. José remained incommunicado for lengthy stretches, periodically shouting out in accompaniment to crude rap lyrics.

While I was disturbed by the misogynistic content of the music, I was even more annoyed by the way José rapped as if there was no one there to hear him. As we paddled around U-bends that diverted for several miles, east and west, before snaking again to the north, I fought off the sense that this whole undertaking was a horrible mistake, a mental trap more likely to obliterate than it was to heal.

Eagles burst from gently shaking cottonwood branches. I had become accustomed to the presence of these magnificent beings over the last couple days. But this evening, in the pink twilight, their presence felt strikingly intimate. Two or three bald eagles at a time alighted and hovered above the canoe, tangling in aerial dance, grabbing hold and spinning, extending their wings and whooshing out of view atop the forest canopy.

It had long been my habit to offer prayers in the presence of eagles. I found comfort in the practice, believing strongly that my prayers were heard, if not always answered. This night, however, my prayers were answered immediately. I looked up at a very large eagle, whose eyes met mine as he flapped two paddle lengths above my head.

How do I heal my broken heart?

In my head I heard a loving voice that I knew belonged to the eagle. *Open your heart to me.*

The river wound into the day's last light, and as night fell I questioned the validity of the encounter with the eagle. I'd heard of animals communicating with humans, but had generally thought these stories metaphorical. If I was to accept what I thought had occurred—that a bird, or a spirit manifesting in a bird, had talked to me—I would have to do away with the assumptions I had been raised with.

I quietly sang an eagle-honoring song I had learned on the Rosebud Reservation, and relaxed for the first time in months. I thought back to the Lakota elders who had told me that eagles live in both the spirit world and the material world; they listen to our prayers and carry them into the universe. I stowed my paddle, kicked my legs up onto the gunwales, and let the moving water carry us forward.

I wasn't ready to tell José about my experience. But that night, camped under a dank bridge some 70 miles south of Grand Forks, he had one of his own. When I couldn't immediately produce the eagle feather from the tent's clutter, he panicked, voicing plans to paddle back to the previous campsite to find it. A minute later, when I unearthed the waterproof case in which I'd stored the feather, José snatched it with the indignation and militancy of a man confronting his oppressor. "If you can't take care of this," he said, "I'll have to keep it with me."

I was puzzled by his knee-jerk possessiveness. José had never been capable of keeping anything; he'd always lived a nomadic existence, moving between the homes of relatives, carrying his clothing in paper bags. Anything he had of value was eventually lost, pawned, stolen, or given away.

Now, José rolled some of the sage I'd brought in a Ziploc between his palms, held a lighter to the grey leafy ball, and placed it in a stainless cup. He smudged the feather, used it to fan smoke over his head and body, and then offered it to me. I cleansed myself in the fragrant swirls while José prayed in the Lakota way, praying to Tunkashila for good health and good help, and asking the great mystery to take pity on him.

GRAND FORKS

The following day, we paddled 36 uneventful river miles. We continued into the evening, and finally reached the point at which I expected to find Grand Forks, or at least to see its city lights. Alas, the banks remained black as interstellar space. It was midnight, and once again—exhausted after 14 hours on the water—José questioned my navigation skills.

"Are you sure you didn't steer us up the wrong river?"

I told him to stop paddling. "Are we going with the current or against it?"

The white concrete tongue of a boat landing on the North Dakota side drifted lazily past the bow.

"With it?" José replied uncertainly.

"River navigation is simple," I said. "So long as we're going in the same direction as the current, we will eventually find the sea."

"Seems too simple, bro. What if we mistakenly turned up one of those streams that flow into this river?"

"We'd know we were going the wrong way because we'd be paddling against the current." He thought about this for a few minutes. Although José would often question my judgment over the remainder of the journey, never again would he question my navigation skills.

According to the map, the Lincoln Park boat landing was supposed to be precisely where we were looking. We considered camping on what appeared to be a lawn, but decided against it. Something seemed off. Our chart led me to believe that Lincoln Park was surrounded by dense residential development. This place was a void, and we hadn't pushed ourselves to midnight to spend another night in the void.

A mile downriver, just as I was beginning to worry that we had somehow missed Grand Forks, I noticed the running lights of a small boat, the first one we'd seen on the waterway. As we approached the anchored vessel, I heard a man cry out, "Whoa, Jesus! What the hell is that? A giant beaver?"

On board, two young men holding fishing rods squinted into the firmament.

"Hey!" I called. "You guys know how far it is to Grand Forks?"

"Are you a giant beaver?" they asked.

We grabbed the rails of the 20-foot Gambler and let them get a good look at us.

They seemed to come to their senses. "Oh, ah, Grand Forks? It's all around us."

They went on to explain that after the flood of 1997, which displaced 60,000 people and indirectly set downtown Grand Forks ablaze, walls were erected that obscured the city from the river. They added that they knew there was a campground "around here somewhere," and they'd be happy to tow us to it. We tied our canoe onto a rear cleat and boarded the two-seat bass boat.

Todd and Scott offered us beers from the two 30-packs chilling in the icy fish well. They'd been on the river all day, they said, "competing in a fishing tournament."

I accepted a cold can from Todd, but José declined, his stomach not yet recovered from the Beefaroni burst.

"Yes!" Todd shouted, pointing in Scott's face. "I'm one up on you now!" Apparently I was on his team.

Scott looked defeated. He explained that the federal government had recently named Grand Forks the binge-drinking capital of the United States. "We won it, dude!" he exclaimed. "And it was because there's nothing else to do here!" Then he stepped onto the top deck, pulled down his basketball shorts, and pissed a long arc into the waterway.

Two sips into my can of Busch Light, Scott shoved another one in my grill. "Come on, dude, you have to help me catch up. It's not fair if you only help him."

In the lexicon of Grand Forks, "fishing tournament" was apparently code for "drinking contest." Apparently these two had challenged each other to polish off a case each. And by the looks of the near empty boxes, they were rounding the final turn and stumbling to a photo finish. Scott chugged a final pull from his can and chucked it into the river.

As we motored along, the fully-loaded canoe trailed behind on a 30-foot length of rope, skidding back and forth across the wake. After five minutes we arrived at what Scott and Todd thought to be the Red River State Recreation Area, a campground established after the flood. They beached the Gambler in the mud beneath a hulking dike, 50 feet from solid earth. It was as close as they could get to shore without ruining their propeller.

José and I struggled through the remaining knee-deep mire, dragging the canoe across its sticky grip one great heave at a time. We lifted packs onto each other's backs, and abandoned the canoe on the mud after it became stubborn, tying it off to a flimsy sage root, our best option for an anchor in case the river were to rise overnight.

The sun was up early the following morning, and in the absence of shade, so was I. Atop the 50-foot dike, I looked out of the tent and saw a long prairie. In light of the suspicion our travels had already engendered along the Red, I wasn't surprised when the distant khaki dot weaving its way through the scrub brush slowly became recognizable as a member of East Grand Forks's finest. José popped up with instinctive panic when I told him who was coming.

The officer tiptoed his way through the thistle field that separated us, holding his pant legs up to prevent the bottoms from touching the earth. This provided us with the time we needed to make our haphazard camp presentable. I met him some way out, hoping he wouldn't come poking around in our stuff.

"You can't stay on the dike. The campground is over there," the cop said gruffly, pointing to an indistinct region of the prairie three football fields away. He insisted on inspecting our illegal settlement and running our names for warrants, then asked José if he used any aliases. In fact, he had many of them—Fifty Dollah, Joe Deala, Joey D, Dizzizo. But now he wisely responded, "Nah, just José."

After José checked out, the zit-faced young cop explained that he would need to inspect our boat. He stood atop the flood wall, scanning the filthy approach to the brown-stained canoe. Following a moment's consideration, he decided it wouldn't be worth soiling his crisp uniform.

It was our first day off after eight days of paddling, but there was work to do. After taking down the tent and reestablishing ourselves under the only tree in the desolate campground, we stuffed a Duluth pack with saturated clothing. Away from the water, the morning was oppressively humid.

We trudged along the craggy sidewalks of East Grand Forks in search of a laundromat. A mile up the valley a pair of golden arches shimmered like an oasis.

The other patrons in line for Sausage McMuffins and Southern Style Chicken Biscuits looked down their noses at us. We were wretched and covered in mud, but we were also entirely unbothered. Having paddled 260 miles already, halfway from the headwaters to the Canadian border, we bathed in the curative air-conditioning with a sense of strength and accomplishment that was only solidified by the disapproving glares.

We found the East Side Laundromat a few long blocks

beyond the McDonald's and hurried inside to coolness and shade. Under the gaze of an elderly gentleman wearing an Indiana Jones fedora, we emptied our clothes into a front loader, then threw in the pack, the socks off our feet, and the shirts off our backs.

José noticed the guy hanging around long after his clothes were folded and placed in the trunk of his Buick. "What's with Old Boy?" he mumbled. "He's kind of creeping me out."

Just then Old Boy ambled over and nodded toward our sloshing laundry. "That's a fancy rucksack," he offered, pointing to our nylon Duluth pack. "In my day the gear was made of dependable canvas."

Perhaps it was his hat, but for some reason I sensed that Old Boy would know how to appreciate a good adventure. We told him about our route to the sea. His eyes glistened and he began to speak of his youthful exploits in the Far North. "When we went up to the Hudson we didn't know what we were getting into," he explained. "We were just kids, had barely paddled a canoe. Back then, the rivers had yet to be fully mapped, so we had to rely on the local Indians, the uncivilized Cree, to help us find our way. There were very few whites in the North Country in those days. There were a few tight spots, the rapids, the cold, and we were lost for a while, but somehow we found our way. It was a good thing we brought a .22 caliber rifle, because we nearly starved up there a couple times, and had to hunt our food."

His recollections of paddling to Hudson Bay reminded

me of the way my grandmother used to talk about her in-volvement in the French Resistance. You couldn't be sure if her use of "we" referred to things she had done personally, or if it applied to the collective experience of those involved in the movement.

Old Boy's story closely mirrored Sevareid's. If he were still alive, Sevareid would have been 95 years old at this time. And judging from the inches of slack dangling from Old Boy's jaw, this advanced age was within his range.

My curiosity about Old Boy prompted a trip that eve-ning to the East Grand Forks Public Library. I learned that he and Sevareid were perhaps not as similar as I had as-sumed initially.

According to FBI files declassified in 1996, Sevareid was under investigation during the 1950s for alleged anti-American activities. He was suspected of having strong tries to communist organizations at the University of Min-nesota in 1945, and in 1947 he was included on a list of people connected with fundraising for Hollywood celebri-ties who had been called to appear before the House Un-American Activities Committee.

A pioneering radio and television journalist, Sevareid was the first to broadcast the fall of France and the French sur-render to Nazi Germany in 1940. Shortly after, he joined Edward R. Murrow in London to report on the Battle of Britain. It was because of his reporting that Sevareid caught the FBI's attention. Later, while serving as head of the CBS Washington bureau (1946–1954), Sevareid was among the earliest critics of Senator Joseph McCarthy's anti-Communist campaign.

I knew well how easy it was to be labeled a communist in that paranoid age. It was not difficult to imagine Sevareid having antifascist sympathies, though, since he'd witnessed firsthand the destruction wrought by fascism in Europe. As I thought more about the man now, I couldn't help but wonder why, given his obvious intelligence and keen sense of history, an older Sevareid never returned to *Canoeing with the Cree*, in order to provide some reflection on where he'd come from. I wondered if his perspective on Natives and Manifest Destiny had changed over the years.

In any case, if the adult Sevareid leaned left, his animated doppelgänger in East Grand Forks was, in José's estimation, "a right-wing wacko." Old Boy warned us that Canada had changed since he roamed the north woods. "You have to be especially careful when it comes to those Mountie bastards," he said. "Don't trust them. Those communists will take the gun right out of your hands. They'll warn you not to go into polar bear territory without a weapon, and then they'll throw you in the slammer for having one."

Changing the subject as our laundry dried, I asked Old Boy if he knew where we could clean up. I hadn't washed my grimy body for a week, and the campground's showers were under construction.

We accepted a ride to the Elks Park swimming pool, a public facility that happened to be adjacent to our campground. As we gathered our belongings from the back seat of the Buick, Old Boy left us with a warning: "Be careful up there!"

We promised the girls at the pool desk we wouldn't take a dip in the pool, and they let us shower without paying the $2.50 entry fee. We must have spent an hour under the bracing jets from those high-pressure spouts, pushing the wall timers every two minutes and scrubbing layers of grime from our bodies with liquid soap from the dispensers.

We dressed in freshly laundered T-shirts and walked across the campground to the sporting goods store. José waited outside. Neither of us had ever purchased a firearm in a store before, and it seemed implausible that we could simply walk in, make our selection, lay down a credit card, and walk out with a gun.

I was a 20-year vegetarian who had refused to shoot when my father took me hunting. I had learned everything I knew about guns from my exchange with Hal back in Saint Paul. Recalling his suggestion, I looked for a 20-gauge shotgun with pump action. I perused the racks slowly, imagining myself unloading into an unfortunate polar bear.

I held a Smith & Wesson and considered my reflection in the mirror behind the counter. No good. I would have needed an L.L. Bean vest and a golden retriever to accompany that preppy weapon.

I tried on a camouflaged Remington. Not the vibe I was looking for. This was a canoe expedition, not a Serbian death squad.

When I pulled an all-black Mossberg SA-20 off the

rack, I knew immediately that it was exactly what I was looking for. Brandishing the shotgun in the mirror, I struck a gangsta pose.

In the two minutes it took to select the Mossberg and carry it to the cash register, I developed a deep and abiding appreciation for my right to bear arms. When the clerk said he would need to hold the SA-20 while he ran a background check, I was indignant.

The clerk noticed. "It'll only take 15 minutes, sir."

Roughly 10 minutes later, I burst out of the store.

At the stagnant mouth of the English Coulee, a drainage ditch that empties into the Red River a few miles north of Grand Forks, the water boiled with dozens of foraging carp. José leaped onto a culvert and dropped a line into the maelstrom. I didn't have the heart to tell him that these invasive pests were not the prized game fish he imagined them to be. When the bottom feeders didn't hit the Shad Rap he was using for bait, José jerked his monofilament through the swarm, snagging one of the whiskered monsters through its yellow underbelly. He yanked the rod skyward and held up the weighty carp, beaming.

When the fish flopped off the treble hook and rejoined the nasty stew, José vowed not to rest until he had settled the score. He repeatedly yanked the razor-barbed bait, but failed to snag another one.

José looked at me menacingly after I convinced him to board and continue our journey to Hudson Bay. "Bro," he sneered, "it's on with these carp bitches."

The 25-mile stretch between Grand Forks and a dot on the Minnesota side called Oslo was an epic battle. The river straightened here, and José and I paddled hard for hours, with José tirelessly smashing the surface wake formed by squadrons of advancing carp. They sped toward us in groups of four to six on either side of the bow. Moments before reaching José they would flare out and nosedive, before bursting from the depths, snarling and spitting, their eyes level with José's.

"Fuck you!" he screamed, swinging his paddle wildly. "Die, motherfuckers!"

After the initial waves of these freshwater kamikazes passed without inflicting the least bit of damage, I grew frustrated with José's obsession. I sighed to the towering clouds, but he refused to paddle until the orange cinder of sun nestled in the treetops, and the carp disappeared along with the light.

Just before nightfall we spotted what looked to be the girders of the Oslo bridge, and the silhouettes of a dozen or so people sitting beneath it. Some were fishing, their legs hanging over a concrete bulwark. Others relaxed on folding chairs. I had grown weary of the scrutiny we'd already encountered on our journey, and, fearing the worst, I thought to pull out and establish camp short of the bridge. But José spoke up with conviction. "Those aren't rednecks," he said. "Those are nice people."

As we glided beneath the trestle in the facing light, I recognized my mistake. These were not the flaxen Scandinavians I had expected of a place called Oslo. Rather, they were Latinos, and their shell-shocked faces and grimy clothing led me to think they had traveled far, and not rested for a very long time.

They returned our greetings with stony silence. One of the men on the bulwark, apparently fearing we were border patrol, turned to the others and hissed, "La Migra. Callate!"

I asked if there was a boat landing nearby. A pregnant young woman answered in a friendly voice. "Over there. Just past the bridge." She was reprimanded by the man beside her with a backhanded swat to the shoulder.

At the landing a lone man stood under the amber sky, casting a line. Unlike his compatriots, Alberto didn't appear to be afraid of us. He spoke perfect English and offered that he was fishing alone because the others didn't like him. José and I would later conjecture that the people under the bridge were likely undocumented migrant workers who preferred to remain out of sight; Alberto fished in the open, perhaps because his documents were straight. As we conversed, the folks who had been fishing beneath the bridge loaded into a windowless cargo van and sped off. I felt sorry we'd spooked them.

After pitching our tent on a patch of grass above the landing, we walked three blocks into town. Built on one of the few hills in the region, Oslo was located unusually close to the river. We surveyed the town's several square blocks and walked past a grocery store, a post office, a bar, and a Ford dealership. But we did not encounter another Mexican.

Another long day on the river had left us weary and

hungry. The only open business in Oslo that night was an American Legion Post. I stopped to tie my shoe, and when I went to enter the dusky club seconds behind José, I ran into him in the doorway, already on his way out. My eyes locked with the bartender's, and I guessed what had upset José. She'd given him the "We don't serve your kind here" look, an expression that melted from her face when she saw me.

The spacious club was empty, except for a handful of elderly men playing cards in a side room. The barstools and some 20 tables were all unoccupied, but when I walked over and asked the bartender if the kitchen was open, she shook her head. "We're closed for a private party. You and your friend will have to leave."

José had consumed nothing all day but a handful or two of trail mix. He was dragging and pale, so I launched a charm offensive, hoping she would relent and stick some pizzas in the toaster oven for us.

It took less than a minute of listening to our story for the ice to start cleaving off the bartender. "That's really interesting," she replied. "My son has always wanted to explore the river. He figures if he followed it all the way he could paddle to the sea. I've always been against it. The Red River is extremely dangerous—deadly undertows, you know. But he just turned 18. I guess I can't really stop him." The bartender's dread of the river reminded me of the unfounded fears people had expressed to Sevareid and Port along their route.

She showed me a satellite photograph of Oslo during the 1997 flood, a tiny island rising from a great lake. "We were surrounded by water," she explained. "The whole town was stranded." I could see how the Red would be a fearsome challenge when it was above flood stage. But when the river remained within its banks, it was a long and winding drainage ditch, cutting through a sea of mud.

The bartender solemnly pulled the cellophane from two pizzas and slid them into the toaster oven. She seemed reflective as she set our Cokes on the bar. The Minnesota Twins were on television, in the bottom of the fifth inning against the Boston Red Sox. She looked up and watched a couple of pitches.

Between innings a news brief showed clips of President Bush's surprise visit to Baghdad. Bush praised Iraqi Prime Minister Nouri al-Maliki for his "efforts to unite Iraq's diverse religious and ethnic groups and end the sectarian attacks that have left thousands dead." Resolute, the commander in chief went on to say that "the Iraqi government must root out corruption at all levels." I tried to suppress my exasperation at the Orwellian notion of President Bush admonishing a foreign government for corruption, but the bartender noticed anyhow.

She confessed that her "damn fool" son, with the encouragement of his father, was about to enlist in the Army, "to fight for that son-of-a-Bush in Iraq."

The timer on the toaster oven dinged.

On her way over to it, the bartender asked how old José was.

"I just had my birthday," he said. "I'm 20."

"My son," she counted on her fingers, "is 14 months younger than you."

José said his brother Juanito, who was 17, had recently joined the Army. A judge in Wisconsin had offered him a choice. "The recruiter told him he'll be in Iraq within six months. Juanito thinks that'll beat going to jail. Some guys can't do time."

The bartender set our steaming trays on the bar. She slid an order pad and pen down the bar and asked me to jot down my email. She said she would encourage her son to write us about our trip. Maybe he would be inspired to skip the war and paddle to Canada instead.

After we had finished our pizza and the baseball game was over, the bartender insisted we follow her into the other room to meet some of the veterans. "I know the boys will get a big kick out of hearing about your trip," she said.

She couldn't have been much older than 40, but she introduced us to the table of veterans like a proud elderly woman presenting her grandchildren. The boys enjoyed hearing about our adventure. Some were familiar with Sevareid's account, and had even considered taking the trip themselves over the years. They wished us Godspeed as we walked to the door, accompanied by the bartender.

"I'm going to have my son write to you. Please get back to him," she added. "He'll be so jealous."

I pledged to return the young man's message, but I never heard from him.

The following morning I sat up in the tent, studying

the map. Tracing my finger over the route from Oslo to the Canadian border induced vertigo—the blue line wound like wet spaghetti in pendulous sweeps and switchbacks. I thought ahead to the killer white water and frigid lakes awaiting us in Canada, along with the possibility of losing our way and starving.

Pushing out of Oslo, we faced a screaming northwesterly gale that would alternately love and hate us for the next three days. When the wind was in our face, we lowered our heads and raged against it, gaining three feet and then blowing back two. José's complaints about pain returned, as did his fantasies of evacuation by helicopter.

One advantage of the strong headwind was that the wildlife never smelled us coming. Around nearly every bend, we encountered deer, eagles, turtles, beaver, wood ducks, and Canadian geese. When we rounded another bend and the tempest shifted to our backs, we'd recline with our boots on the gunwales, turning our faces to the sun with closed eyes.

Like a toxic relationship, this dynamic of soaring heights and bruising lows made for a dizzying slog. Out of Oslo we paddled four and a half miles over two hours, only to end up a mile north of where we began.

After some 35 miles we arrived, exhausted, at the green girders of the Highway 17 bridge. The state of North Dakota maintained a gauging station here, atop a neatly mowed hill. We set camp on the plush grass at sunset, angering a great buck that stepped out of the trees, stomping and snorting at us for encroaching on his meadow. Too drained to cook and wash dishes, I boiled a pan of water and heated a pouch of curry sauce, then tore it open and ate it with a spoon. José pulled the top off his final can of Beefaroni and sat under the sparkling Milky Way, dipping saltines into the tepid goo.

In the morning I was pleased to find that José had cleaned up after his meal for a change. All the pots were put away and the food barrel was sealed tight. But a few miles into the blistering day, taking advantage of a tailwind to scrounge around for a handful of trail mix, I touched something clammy in the food barrel and withdrew my hand to find it covered in bloody Beefaroni. José had stashed his dirty dishes without washing them.

Just then we arrived at the end of the straightaway, where the Tamarac River enters the Red. A blast furnace gust stopped us in our tracks, forcing me to paddle furiously with my slimy hand in order to avoid being blown into a tangle of cottonwoods enmeshed across the mouth of the tributary.

The distraction gave me a moment to consider my words before taking it up with José. We'd spent 12 days together as constant companions—eating, sleeping, and paddling in tight quarters—and had not yet exchanged a word in anger. We were having fun most of the time, and getting to know each other much better with each passing day.

Watching José adjust to life on the river, I was learning the true meaning of what it means to be adaptable. He came to the trip with little know-how and barely any gear, and yet he submitted to the monotonous regimen. It wasn't originally his dream to paddle to Hudson Bay, and yet he complained only occasionally about the pain. And even then, he would put his paddle in the water.

"Dude," I said, my initial level of annoyance tempered by the reflection, "you put the fucking dishes in the food barrel without washing them."

"Oh, hell no," he laughed, noticing that the shaft of my paddle was painted Beefaroni red. "My bad."

We soldiered on through this torturous stretch, exhausting our drinking water 10 miles out of Drayton, on the hottest and most humid day of the summer. The river was grotesquely serpentine. At one bend we viewed the round tops of the Drayton Grain Elevator. It couldn't have been more than a half mile north of us as the crow flies, but the river refused to take us there. The channel curved abruptly east and sent us through a hellish five-mile labyrinth before leading back toward town. We deployed our water purification system, but after just a few pumps the filter clogged with silt. My tongue swelled.

José asked impatiently about Drayton.

"Will there be a McDonald's? Will there be hos?"

My dehydrated brain envisioned Drayton with all the bells and whistles of a modern city. I confirmed that there would be a McDonald's. Probably hos, too.

When we finally arrived at the Drayton boat landing, we found little more than torn and faded banners on electrical posts. They proclaimed the town the "Catfish Capital of the North," and led us up a potholed hill.

The streets were empty. The only apparent businesses, a post office and a grocery store, were closed. We walked down the two-block main street, a yawning business district whose heyday had long since passed, and into a quaint residential neighborhood distinguished by small, well-kept homes, campy lawn ornaments, and the stench of hog manure.

Suddenly José and I looked at each other. We'd picked up the unmistakable sound of Kanye West's "Jesus Walks"—faintly at first, then booming, as the pickup truck from which it emanated approached from behind us. We flagged down the truck, and a toothless white guy with greasy blond locks cranked down his window and asked how he could help. A bulky plastic crucifix dangled from his rear view, and half a cigarette from his lip. In a voice that sounded much older than his appearance would have suggested, he said there was only one restaurant in town, a drive-in about a mile up Main. If we hoofed it really fast, he added, we might make it before the place closed. Then he peeled off abruptly, bumping into the curb before he was back on his way.

After taking our orders, the cute young waitress at Andy's Drive-In sat down next to José. "What the hell is wrong with you guys?"

"What do you mean?" I asked.

"You look like you've been through hell. Your face is

peeling off and your lips are cracked and bleeding," she said.

She was the only server on duty, and all seven tables were occupied. And yet this young lady who introduced herself as Tiffany somehow managed to keep everyone happy and steal time to pepper us with questions. She was about José's age, but she paid no attention to him. José's competitive spirit surfaced as we finished our ice cream. He took to calling me "the old guy." "Hey Tiffany," he said at one point, "would you mind getting him some more water? I don't want the old guy getting dehydrated."

Tiffany introduced us to the cook as he wadded up his apron and tossed it on the kitchen floor. He told us about a campground that had showers. It was far from the boat landing, but he agreed to drive us to the canoe and then back up to Schumacher Park.

As we were leaving, Tiffany handed me a slip of paper with her address. "I'm going to be worried until I hear from you. You have to promise to write. Just let me know you're alive."

"I'll make sure the old guy drops you a line," José replied.

As we walked out to the cook's Taurus, I wasted no time giving him shit for his bad behavior. "You son of a bitch!" I hissed. He wasn't able to respond in the car, but I saw José's face drop. He thought I was serious.

The cook stuck his nose out the window. "Smell that?" he asked. "Whenever there's a north wind this whole town stinks of sugar beets. I don't normally notice, but on days like this, you can't help it."

I knew the stench of manure well. I once lived in Aurora, South Dakota, across the street from a hog confinement. The smell coming from the sugar factory was identical to the way my daughters' hair used to smell when they came inside from playing.

We soon learned that the cook was a senior at Drayton High School. He didn't know what he was going to do after graduation, but he figured he would probably end up "fishing cats" and working at American Crystal Sugar, one of the region's biggest employers of Drayton's low-skilled youth.

José brooded as he helped set the tent between two RVs at Schumacher Park. The brief flirtation with Tiffany had left him hot and bothered. He concocted scenarios involving Tiffany and her friends coming into our camp for the night.

I was unmoved by the encounter with the young waitress. After my divorce I had come to see almost any kind of involvement with women as a one-way street to emotional desolation.

"How do you expect me to meet women when you look like that?" José asked. He had been after me for a few days to shave my unruly beard.

I said I thought women liked scruffy men.

"Hell no," he replied.

I had only one razor and my beard was so thick that I removed less than half of it under a cold shower before the blades dulled. Early the next morning, sporting islands of hair in an archipelago stretching from my cheek to my neck, I walked into town and waited for the grocery store to open. I bought two razors, and walked through the meat department to the bathroom. It took a while to scrape away all the stubble, and when I finished I felt raw and exposed.

José was pleased. "Now you don't look like an old man."

I said I thought women liked older men.

"Hell no," he replied again.

When we returned to Andy's for breakfast, Andy himself opened the door for us.

"You must be the intrepid voyageurs paddling to the Bay!"

Andy took our order, cooked our pancakes and omelets, served them with coffee and juice, and then sat down with us. He said the whole town was abuzz: "I've been open three hours and all I've heard about is those kids going north! You guys are celebrities!" Andy refused payment for breakfast and offered us a lift back to our camp.

We packed up, double-checked the site to make sure we weren't leaving anything behind, and humped our gear a mile back to the landing.

As we paddled around the first bend and put Drayton behind us, José spoke up cheerfully. "Hudson Bay, nigga!"

To which I replied, "Hudson Bay!"

Three hours after I had plugged my phone into the solar charger, we were shocked when it rang. It was Homegirl J, calling for José. I slipped to my knees and handed the phone up to the bow.

Homegirl J wanted to know where José's brother was. "I let D hold my drugs and I haven't seen him in two days." I could hear her whine from back in the stern.

José broke it down for her: "Are you stupid? Never let D hold your shit."

When he finished I asked José what was up.

"She called because she wants dick," he said. "She's coming to meet us in Winnipeg. This broad's rich with that casino per cap. We'll get a nice hotel room with two queen beds and a couple bottles."

If all went well at the border, we would be in Winnipeg in just a few days. I said I didn't think it was such a great idea to have Homegirl J come up. I feared she would take José home with her.

"It's all good, bro," José replied. "I told her to bring a broad for you."

CROSSING THE BORDER

Twenty-five river miles north of Drayton, José and I were joking around about people back home, as we often did. My friend Greeny's strict adherence to the law was the subject on this occasion. Greeny had borrowed the canoe one time the previous year. Before taking it, he purchased permit stickers from the Department of Natural Resources and affixed them to the boat. José and I found it amusing that Greeny went to the trouble and expense of complying with a regulation that would never be enforced.

"These waters belong to the people," I said. "This river was here before America and it will be here long after. The government has no right to charge us for the right to paddle on it."

"Hell no they don't. Greeny must be a chump to pay for those stupid-ass stickers."

Just as José uttered these words, a powerboat manned by two sheriff's deputies outfitted in blaze orange roared around the bend behind us. They throttled back and bobbed on their own wake, watching us through binoculars from some 50 yards off. Before long, their boat eased up alongside us, the unmistakable scent of Old Spice filling the air.

The last boat landing we'd passed was in Drayton. These guys had to have motored at least 25 miles to track us down. I wondered what had made them so curious.

They maintained their aggressive posture even after they spied Greeny's permit stickers.

"I see you're up to date," said one of them.

The other man began reciting the Minnesota angling code. *All people 16 years and older need a license. To purchase a noncommercial game or fish license, nonresidents and residents must have their social security number on file with DNR or must provide it*—only to recognize that we were not fishing. Fortunately, I had stashed our pole earlier. Needless to say, we had never purchased a fishing license.

When the water police zoomed away after just a few minutes, José tracked them closely, like a little boy watching a jumbo jet draw its course across the wide blue sky. "Damn," he mused, "if we had one of them jet boats we'd be at Hudson Bay in a quick minute."

I was relieved to have negotiated yet another run-in with the law, and thankful that Greeny had the foresight to purchase the permits. But this initial response quickly gave way to renewed indignation.

"Fuck them bitches," I said angrily. "They have no right to come out here and interrogate us."

"They are bitches," José replied thoughtfully. "But that boat, bro, that boat made the canoe look like a bitch. I ain't gonna lie, bro, that police boat was dope. Did you see you how fucking fast they went?"

I recognized in my own strong reaction to these authority figures something more often associated with indigenous people: a sense of deep connection to the earth that results from moving over it under one's own power, while drawing deep meaning from the creatures and elements encountered along the way. Over the past two weeks we had paddled to the upper reaches of the Red River, giving blood, sweat, and tears along the way. In contrast to these soft officers, with their aluminum badges and pressed khakis, we felt instinctively that the river was our home. The police felt like colonizers.

This brief interaction brought to mind teachings shared with me by a spiritual leader of the Midewiwin Lodge on the Bad River Reservation in northern Wisconsin. In a longhouse made of lashed maple branches, on the south shore of Lake Superior, he recited the seven fires prophecy of the Ojibwe. What came to mind now was the fourth fire prophecy, delivered originally by a pair of prophets some three centuries before white men first encountered the Ojibwe people.

The first prophet said,

You will know the future of our people by the face the light-skinned race wears. If they come wearing the face of brotherhood, then there will come a time of wonderful change for generations to come. This will bring new knowledge and articles that can be joined with the knowledge of this country. In this way, two nations will join to make a mighty nation. This new nation will be joined by two more so that four will form the mightiest nation of all. You will know the face of brotherhood if the light-skinned race comes carrying no weapons, if they come bearing only their knowledge and a handshake.

And the other prophet said,

Beware if the light-skinned race comes wearing the face of death. You must be careful because the face of brotherhood and the face of death look very much alike. If they come carrying a weapon, beware. If they come in suffering, they could fool you. Their hearts may be filled with greed for the riches of this land. If they are indeed your brothers, let them prove it. Do not accept them in total trust. You shall know that the face they wear is one of death if the rivers run with poison and fish become unfit to eat. You shall know them by these many things.

In these officers—with their Tasers, their sidearms, and their hostile attitudes—I saw a representation of the face of death. I looked down at the heavily polluted river. It seemed unmistakably true that the worst possible outcome foreseen in the fourth prophecy had come to fruition here on the Red River.

The Highway 175 boat ramp and the drive leading to it were lined with large mudbanks that could only have been created by a massive snowplow. We made camp after a 28-mile day on a cracked mud field adjacent to the landing.

There was an hour of daylight remaining, and José seemed determined to take full advantage of it. He unzipped the gun bag and posed like Scarface with the Mossberg, extending the long-barreled weapon at the end of his lanky arm and popping imaginary caps on "that nigga Sonic." He begged me to tell him where I had put the ammo.

I resisted, concerned that José wouldn't be satisfied until both boxes of slugs had been wasted, leaving us with none when we needed them most. And when I refused to let him remove the materials the manufacturer had installed in the chambers for safe shipping, he got salty and said he was "going to town to find something to do." There was no town, but he would not be dissuaded.

I followed him onto the Highway 175 overpass and down a sweeping stretch of road that joined purple virga at the edge of the horizon. A mile into the misadventure, José gave up and walked back with me through a thick evening haze that loomed over the immense landscape.

Back in the tent, I continued the nightly ritual I'd established early in the mission. If I wasn't studying the map or paging through *Canoeing with the Cree*, I rested on my back, making an impression in the mud. I prayed for my children and for José, and gave thanks for the relief resulting from grueling days on the water.

I drifted off to dream of flying up the sun-soaked river valley, an eagle above the water, at the height of the treetops. I felt the wind press against the downy feathers on my forehead as I soared along the sweeping shoreline. It was a weightless pleasure I'd never known before.

"Bro, wake up!" I recognized José's voice immediately. "There are rednecks out there."

I could hear a vehicle idling nearby, and when I poked my head out of the tent I saw a darkened pickup parked at the bottom of the ramp, near the water's edge. The presence of the truck, and the two figures outlined in the cab, didn't alarm me. In fact, I was pretty certain they didn't even know we were there. But José was sure "they were coming to rape and kill us." He was genuinely panicked, and demanded the gun. I refused, handing him the filet knife from our tackle box instead, to calm his nerves. He pulled the eight-inch blade under his sleeping bag and hugged it like a teddy bear. Curled into a ball, he fixed his eyes on the tent flap, poised to attack at the slightest movement.

Following an entirely uneventful night, I awoke the following morning wracked with anxiety. The border was just 25 miles away. I had crossed into Canada many times by canoe, but not since 9/11, and certainly not while carrying a weapon in the company of a young man with a long rap sheet. Unable to roust José, I paged through *Canoeing with the Cree*, hoping it might offer some guidance.

In Sevareid's day the Red River was heavily trafficked by steamships hauling passengers and freight between Fargo and Winnipeg. There was a customs post on the border, and according to Sevareid's account, the officials stationed there declared the pair the first to pass that port of entry by canoe. "We did not, however, get through without paying a deposit of five dollars and a quarter," he wrote, "which would be returned if we came back with the canoe." Once these formalities had been concluded, Sevareid and Port took the inspector out for a short paddle, "at the end of which he was forced to go ashore on the shoulders of Walt, because of the mud."

As we approached the border, I was increasingly uptight. I made precautionary lists in preparation for the inspection, and insisted that José take his headphones off and comply with my directives: "Remove anything that might lead them to think you're a gang member. No bandannas, no red or black hats, and no tank tops. You might want to put on something that looks outdoorsy."

In fact, José was perhaps the only male in his family who was not affiliated with a gang. His cousins wore the colors of many street crews: Crips, Bloods, Latin Kings, Vice Lords, and Native Mob. Their primary allegiance was to one another, however, though this didn't stop law enforcement from harassing José and the other men in his family.

A few miles south of Pembina, North Dakota, the tension was interrupted by a phone call from D. José listened for several minutes with a quiet intensity that made me think his mother had died. Then he burst out laughing, rolling onto the Duluth packs with his legs in the air and shouting joyously, "That nigga Sonny finally got his. And I thought that niggie Makoce was getting soft."

José went on to explain that he and his cousin Makoce had been waiting for two years to get revenge on Sonny, whom he described as "this nigga from Frogtown that fucks with Makoce's sister Terra." The previous night, I gathered, Makoce had bumped into Sonny coming out of Terra's house.

"Makoce ran up on Sonny with a bat and put him in a coma. He's hanging on for dear life now," José laughed. "Makoce caught him slipping, and Sonny got what was coming to him. Just when I thought Makoce was getting soft." I had seen José through some very good times, but I couldn't recall having seen him more happy.

We docked in Pembina, hoping for a reprieve from the merciless sun. As we walked past a marker for historic Fort Daer, site of the earliest white settlement in Dakota Territory—where, beginning in the 1790s, French fur traders intermarried with Anishinaabe and Cree women and established the Métis culture—José expounded on the events that had caused the beef with Sonny.

"It all began just before New Year's, 2004, when I was 18," he explained. "I was partying over at Terra's house when Sonny's brother Jason got into it with Terra and ended up busting her lip. Then I got into it with Jason, and he thought he could just roll over on me because this nigga's a huge Indian, like a football player, and I'm a little guy. So Makoce comes through and tries to break things up. Just then, Sonny shows up and thinks Makoce and I are ganging up on Jason. So Sonny pulls out a knife and stabs

Makoce in the neck. Then I pull out the screwdriver I'm carrying in my pocket and stab Jason in the neck."

After a 15-minute walk down the only road we could see from the shoreline, José celebrated the news of Sonny's demise at the Gastrak convenience mart, with two micro-waved cheeseburgers, a sack of Flamin' Hot Cheetos, and a Monster energy drink. He couldn't stop talking about Sonny's beating on the walk back as well. Justice was obviously intoxicating for him.

Back at the Red River, I searched Fort Daer Recreation Area for a place to stash my contraband before we set out to cross the border. I had decided that the stress associated with carrying weed across the border outweighed its potential benefits. As I surveyed the grounds of the old fort—now a baseball field, campground, and playground—I thought briefly with envy of the Voyageurs who once settled here.

I fell to my knees in the grass and removed the Ziploc bag from my day pack, intending to leave it buried beneath a flat rock between the baseball field and the flood dike. Before I could do so, however, three husky white men wearing ball caps and vests bearing the insignia of the local citizens' patrol appeared on four-wheel ATVs atop the dike, some 30 yards away. While they surveyed the scene, I stashed the sack in my day pack, marched to a nearby outhouse, and dumped it down the dark hole.

When I emerged into daylight, the flabby vigilantes, now six strong, silent and immovable, were parked on the trail between me and the docks, watching the outhouse door. I walked past without acknowledging them. They regarded me suspiciously, but allowed me to pass over the flood barrier unhindered.

José and I had intended to spend the night in the Fort Daer campground and set out for Canada in the morning. It would soon be dark, massive thunderheads were piling above the plains to our west, and we had no idea where we might find another campsite when we did cross the border. Still, José's expression on my return said in no uncertain terms that there was no way he was staying in Pembina. We shoved off under the watchful eye of the four-wheeled spies, their ATVs in single file atop the dike.

As we paddled out of town, we could hear the distant rumble of trucks shifting gears. Between silhouettes of weeping willows, we saw the glow cast by floodlights at the Pembina/ Emerson border post, a mile or so in from the muddy banks. But there was no customs station here on the Red River, no sign of welcome to "Friendly Manitoba." The border was marked by nothing more than a black trestle of crisscrossed girders, and as we slipped along undocumented beneath the railroad span, we were aided by a welcome rush of current, the first significant natural flow we'd experienced since beginning the trip 400 river miles to the south.

We hadn't planned to sneak into Canada, but it seemed foolish to disembark and walk to the customs station. And so we chose the path of least resistance, paddling across the swirling waters in shimmering twilight. José expressed relief. It had been his idea from the start to steal across the border under the cover of night. "Fuck them border bitches," he laughed. "Them bitches can't touch us out here."

For the first time in two weeks, we could see a mile into the future. The river, which had been infuriatingly serpentine to this point, suddenly straightened. Though the last daylight was fading, I was eager to keep moving, to dig in and put some distance between us and the border.

José had other ideas. This was the first time he had traveled outside the United States, and he wanted to mark the occasion with a few Captain and Cokes, his signature cocktail. José was legal to drink for the first time in his life, and he intended to stop at the first bar we could find.

The map showed a town called Emerson just across the border. A few blighted warehouses rose above the floodwall to our right, but it wasn't particularly inviting. José paddled furiously toward the eastern bank, but without my cooperation he was never going to get there in the swift current. I convinced him that we would find a more suitable place for his first legal drink a few miles downstream.

José soon saw things my way, not least because it was an exceptionally magical evening. Massive thunderheads the color of Dreamsicles piled thousands of feet into the sky around us, every few minutes releasing a downburst of warm wind and precipitation. Around sunset we saw a bobcat scale the trunk of a tall birch, saw the violent shaking of its branches, and heard the terrible cries of the birds whose nest had been raided. This was José's first impression of Canada.

"Damn, nigga," he said earnestly. "It's real out here."

Some five river miles past the border, we were off the road map I'd been using for navigation. I was well prepared to navigate the far north, but for the next 200 miles I had only a common gas station map to go by, and for the stretch between Emerson and Winnipeg I had only the poorly detailed and antiquated descriptions in *Canoeing with the Cree*. It was impossible to get lost on the river, and I knew Winnipeg was no more than a hundred river miles ahead. But I couldn't reliably tell José where we might find alcohol along the way.

Before long we paddled past a couple of dudes in ragged baseball caps. They were fishing from shore for meaty channel cats. There was a "beverage room" up ahead, they said in response to our question. "Stop at the bridge about seven miles downriver. The town of Letellier is a three-mile walk to the west."

The fishermen offered José a Molson from their cooler, but he declined. That wasn't how he envisioned his first legal sip of alcohol. He wanted to be carded properly, and then served a Captain and Coke.

The evening calmed into a warm night, the black canopy above sliced in half by the glowing Milky Way. We came upon the bridge around midnight and, with the aid of headlamps, found a dry rock on which to disembark.

We tied off the canoe and set up camp. José pulled on a sweatshirt and started making his way through the tall grass, up to the bridge deck. "You coming to drink with me, dawg, or what?" he yelled back.

I followed him up to the road. It was strange and exciting to emerge from the river and see road signs in English and French. Earlier that day we had been paddling the Red River. Now were on la rivière Rouge. I squinted into the darkness. There were two or three distant twinkles of light to the west, but nothing that would indicate an active human settlement. I persuaded José to wait until morning for his excursion.

José stayed up that night, pulling hairs from his chin in preparation for the big day to come. Later, he turned out his headlamp and went to sleep without begging me to let him sleep with the shotgun. We were both tired and thrilled to have made it to Canada, a serious milestone on our route to the Bay.

"Good night, nigga," José said drowsily.

"Good night," I replied.

t was usually a chore to get José going in the morning. After some unsuccessful cajoling, I often began taking down the tent while he was still inside.

"Shit, bro," he would whine, "you know I have a process. Just give me a few minutes."

Occasionally I told him it was nine o'clock when it was really seven. But that morning, with the promise of legal alcohol on his mind, José was up and stuffing his clothes away as the tent glowed orange at first light. I was eager to make Winnipeg—still a good three days' paddle away—but I also knew that it would be impossible to convince José to wait for his drinks. So I offered to stay back, take down the tent, and pack our gear, reminding José as he left camp to take his rain gear and a two-way radio.

Three hours later, nasty black thunderheads erupted overhead. I sat shivering under the bridge, wrapped in a tarp as rain slashed me in horizontal streaks. José was not responding on the two-way. Either he had traveled beyond the three-mile range of the radios, or he was simply ignoring me. I finally decided to go after him.

I tried to thumb a ride in the downpour, but the few cars that passed didn't slow down. After I had walked about two miles, José finally responded on the radio. "Bro, I'm crunk as hell! Come down here, man. The place is called Barnay's or some shit, and the bartender is smokin' hot. Hell yeah, dawg." I was irritated.

As I approached the prairie town of Letellier, a tidy collection of buildings that included a grain elevator and two modest brick motels with adjoining beverage rooms, I spotted a slender figure stumbling toward me. I followed José back to Barnay's, where I watched *Canadian Idol* on television, ate a veggie burger, and drank a Moosehead. José downed a third Captain and Coke and ogled the bartender shamelessly.

An hour later the sky began to clear and José and I headed back to camp. I had been hoping that we could still make meaningful river miles that day, but when we reached the bridge we discovered that someone had rifled through our gear, which I had left neatly stored under a tarp at the base of a concrete piling. The only thing missing was the one piece of equipment we could not replace in Canada: our shotgun.

Initially this was a more sobering development for José than it was for me, given his overwhelming fear of bears and white people. Based on more than 25 years of experience in the wilderness—including considerable time in Alaska's grizzly territory—I knew the gun was a precaution, and we probably wouldn't have occasion to use it. But as we loaded the canoe and prepared to shove off, I was struck with a sobering realization. There was a smuggled shotgun on the loose, registered in my name. I could be liable for any crimes that might be committed with that weapon, unless I reported it stolen. But if I were to report the gun stolen, I would have to admit that we had entered the country illegally.

"You boys need some help?" called a friendly voice from the bridge above.

José looked up at the twentysomething man on a bike. "You Indian?" he inquired.

They had a brief exchange, establishing that our new friend was "Canadian Ojibwe."

"We Lakota were the last holdouts against the United States. We killed Custer," José boasted. He repeated this to every Native individual we met along the way, and it invariably elicited bouts of laughter.

After a few moments of internal deliberation, I bit the bullet. The guy on the bridge had a cell phone. I asked him to dial the authorities. Minutes later an officer from the Dakota Ojibwe Police Service came striding down from the road.

Because we were paddling without a good map, I hadn't realized that we were on the Roseau River First Nation Reserve. After I explained the situation—"We meant to pass customs, but there was nowhere to check in!"—the officer told José to "sit tight with the canoe" and ordered me to follow him to his squad car. I climbed into the back seat.

The town of Ginew was made up of several small

shuttered buildings and a cigarette store. It was a two-minute drive from the bridge, and it appeared to be the reserve's center of commerce and government. The officer led me into a rusting building and locked the steel door behind us.

At his desk, in a small office across the hallway from two jail cells, the officer pulled some forms from a drawer and gravely scribbled notes while I described what had happened to the shotgun. He was entirely humorless, so I resorted to complimenting the children in the photos on his desk.

"Those are the sergeant's kids," he grunted.

I had initially hoped this Native officer might concur with my sense that there was nothing wrong with crossing from the United States into Canada unannounced. After all, many indigenous peoples had been divided by the establishment of the arbitrary border. But his body language wasn't encouraging.

Then his phone rang. He answered it on speaker.

"You have to come right away," a panic-stricken woman pleaded. "My son-in-law is walking down to the river with a rope. He said he's going to kill himself."

The officer calmly gathered the caller's information, then got up to leave. "I have to take this. I'm the only one working today. Can you walk back to the bridge and wait there? I'm going to call an officer from the Royal Canadian Mounted Police to meet you." He twisted the dead bolt on the door and turned me loose.

Back at the bridge, I repeated my story to Constable James of the RCMP. He was an imposing presence—six-foot-five or so and barrel-chested in his bulletproof vest—but he seemed to be genuinely intrigued by our expedition. Still, he arrested us, confined us to the back seat of his Explorer, and said we would have to leave our equipment in the canoe while he hauled us back to the border for questioning. We had no choice but to agree, though there was no way to know if there would be anything left of the gear upon our return.

It felt strange to roll along at 60 miles an hour after two weeks on the river. José was visibly mystified by my ongoing exchange with Constable James, conducted through the metal grille that separated us. He sat directly behind James and gestured as if to say, "Why the hell are you talking to a pig? Are you fucking nuts?" But I went on trying to humanize the situation. After 10 minutes we had covered the same distance we traveled by canoe the previous night.

We followed Constable James into the border post, where his deskbound countrymen gawked at the captured American canoeists. A pretty young woman at the currency exchange desk seemed to be particularly interested in what the cop had dragged in. As we sat down in the lobby, José returned her gaze before sliding on his "stunner shades" and kicking back like a cool dude.

"Keep your head in the game," I whispered sharply. "The next few minutes are going to make or break this trip."

"Shit, dawg," José replied defiantly. "If I'm gonna go out, I'm goin out like a G."

Before long Constable James directed us to a desk, behind which sat a stone-faced woman. Her name tag read "Nancy." She too wore a bulletproof vest, which I found surprising given the near nonexistence of gun violence in Canada.

Nancy stood behind her desk, looking at us with black eyes that tolerated no bullshit. Despite her no-nonsense professionalism, I repeated the well-worn falsehood. "We expected a customs station," I said, "or at the very least a sign alerting us to the fact that we were crossing the border. As soon as we realized where we were, and that our gun had been stolen, we called the authorities."

Constable James shuffled behind Nancy, notepad in hand, scribbling throughout my charm offensive. Nancy shot him a look that seemed aimed at marking her jurisdiction. Then she told James there was a drunk driver outside, suggested he make himself useful, and turned her attention back to us. She demanded I sit down so she could question José. I glanced at José's ashen face before abandoning him to Nancy. Settled across the lobby in a hard plastic chair, I looked on helplessly while she interrogated him.

As I watched the two of them talk, I brainstormed next steps. I wasn't going home. If they deported us, we would sneak back across the 4000-mile frontier. There was no point going home until we'd reached Hudson Bay. I resolved to walk if I had to.

When he collapsed next to me on the bench, José was pale and sweaty. "Damn," he uttered breathlessly.

"That broad chopped me up something nasty. Looks like Canada don't want no more Indians up here. They're sendin' me back to Frogtown where a nigga belongs, I already know."

Nancy huddled along the wall near the currency exchange girl, talking in hushed tones with Constable James and a second border agent. When they noticed us looking in their direction, Nancy ushered the small group across the lobby, where they disappeared through an unmarked door.

Constable James popped out a minute later, and came over to us with an update: "They're going to call together the post managers and decide what to do with you. I'll wait here to provide a lift back to the bridge, in case they give the go-ahead."

"What if they decide against us?" I asked. "Will we get our canoe back?"

James explained that if we were deported we would be placed on the next bus to the States. We would never see our canoe again. "Whatever Indian stole your gun has probably helped himself to the rest of your gear," he said. "Some no-good characters around there. You guys chose a very bad place to leave your things."

James's assumption that it was an Indian who had stolen our gun was both irritating and plausible. José registered his displeasure with a silent glance in my direction, then went on to explain to me in hushed tones that Nancy had questioned him about his criminal record, the true nature of our relationship, and whether I was planning to write about the trip. I took this last point to be somewhat promising. My experience as a journalist had led me to understand that people in positions of authority often fear being exposed. And it seemed reasonable to assume that Nancy would think twice before creating a public relations issue.

By the time she and three other bulletproofed officers rejoined us, José had already planned his first moves back in the city. "I'm funna go to Speedy Mart, get me some chili cheese fries, a burger, potato wedges, and a Red Bull," he proclaimed. "And then I'm funna look up some hos, hook up some Coronas, call together my niggas for the update, and get on with makin' fetti."

Nancy motioned for us to stand before her desk. She started to say something in a scolding tone, but she was quickly interrupted by a hairy bear of a bald man, whom I took to be her superior. He seized control of the proceedings.

"Jonathan David Lurie and José Baptiste Perez, the two of you have embarked on an ambitious journey into the great wide unknown," he began with astonishing gravitas. "In the magnificent tradition of explorers and adventurers from throughout the ages, from Marco Polo to Ponce de León, from Leif Erikson to Eric Sevareid," the latter spoken with a knowing wink, "you have undertaken a bold and significant voyage, whose risks and rewards are many, and whose stories will live in the memories of one and all." He paused briefly, then went on. "It is with great pleasure that we, the guardians of the North and royal subjects of Canada, welcome you to our land, and wish you a safe and fulfilling journey, as you paddle the waters of this vast country, across the territory once known as Rupert's Land."

Upon completing this extraordinary oration, the hairy officer held out his arms as if to indicate that the gates to the North had been thrown open. The entire contingent of security officials then shook our hands warmly and wished us safe travels.

On the drive back to the river, Constable James allowed me to sit up front. José remained silent in back, sobered by the unlikely turn of events, and seemingly disappointed that our expedition would continue.

We found the canoe where we'd left it, tied to a rock under the Letellier bridge. Our gear remained unmolested and out of sight beneath the spray deck. With just a few minutes of daylight remaining, we pitched the tent for a second night on the Roseau River Reserve.

Once we were settled in, an uncomfortable silence gripped our muggy domicile. When he did speak, José's voice hardened with the machismo edge that often surfaced when he felt embarrassed or threatened. He was focused now on Winnipeg. He wanted to call Homegirl J, to arrange for her to meet us, but my phone was dead again. He went on to revisit the various ways he was planning to make money back in Frogtown. He described a scheme to work the margins in diamonds, by buying from one pawnshop and selling to another, where his friends worked. Or perhaps he would establish a toe-hold in the tool resale business, which had been lucrative for D for many years. It was increasingly clear that José was fomenting a plot to abandon our mission and return home with Homegirl J.

While I wrote in my journal, capturing what I could remember of the episode at the border post, José fell asleep. I wasn't far behind him, but the unmistakable rumble of an ATV roused us long before sunrise. Before I could even open the fly, its driver shouted, "Hey, the river's rising! Your canoe is floating away!"

I leaped up and darted out into the rain, the chilly mud squishing between my toes. I ran down to find the canoe resting solidly in a couple inches of water, lodged between several large rocks, exactly where we had secured it. I turned to respond to the ATV invader, but he was already spinning his wheels, roaring out of camp.

José was poised at the edge of the tent when I returned. Wide-eyed, he offered his interpretation of what had just happened: "That white kid probably stole our gun. You know he made up a story about the water rising to see if anyone was in the tent so he could steal more of our shit."

An hour or so later, I peeked out of the tent. The sky had cleared, so I walked up to the bridge and plugged my phone into our solar charger. I sat down on the rusty trestle, waiting for the sun to give it life.

In the time it took for me to ingest the gravel kicked up by three semis, the cell ignited. I dialed Ron, a barge captain I'd discovered while researching our route. In Sevareid's day Lake Winnipeg was traversed by passenger ships and freighters on a regular schedule, all 245 miles from Winnipeg to Norway House. But now the only commercial operation on the big lake was Ron and his barge. And according to the secretary at Good Branson Transfer Company, whom I'd reached from Saint Paul, Ron "only goes when it makes sense," and "absolutely never takes passengers."

This time Ron answered my call. He said he was leaving in three days. In order to catch on with him, we'd have to "haul ass to Selkirk," a town on the Red River some 20 miles north of Winnipeg that was home to the barge service. But he would only be able to take our canoe and gear. We'd have to get ourselves to his last stop at Berens River, an Anishinaabe reserve two-thirds of the way up Lake Winnipeg.

That was too complicated, and too expensive. I had envisioned pitching a tent on the deck of the barge and cruising the lake for five days. But Ron explained that we wouldn't be covered under his insurance. I pleaded, countering that we had paddled 400 miles without insurance, and were just fine. To no avail.

José had been sound asleep when I crawled out of the tent an hour earlier, but now he was gone without a trace. I imagined him walking to the pay phone in Letellier and calling Homegirl J. I could see him in the front seat of her Hummer, riding home to Frogtown.

I searched around the empty sleeping bags and found José's water pack and CD player. He'd be back. Then, just as I was packing the last of our gear into the canoe, I heard a C-Murder rap coming from the bridge. José was tamping a pack of cigarettes into his palm as he walked into camp.

"Check out these fucked-up Canadian squares," he said. "They got some messed-up pictures on them."

The packaging was dominated by a gruesome photograph. Two black arrows labeled "lung cancer" pointed to black growths on slick pink tissue.

"You wanna know what's even more messed up, bro? At the Indian smoke shop up there, where they give a Native brother a break, these squares still cost 10 bucks. Ain't that a bitch."

I was furious that José had spent the last of his money on cigarettes. He responded defensively, justifying the purchase by explaining that "at least they got 25 in these packs. Back in the States, you only get 20."

I was already upset about the day before, how he had got drunk and caused us to waste an entire day dealing with the authorities. Now he had spent the last of his money on smokes, and I was increasingly certain that he was aiming to bolt when we reached Winnipeg. But I didn't say anything as we got in the canoe and dipped our paddles for the first time in nearly two days. I knew that if we started arguing now the entire journey would unravel, and we would end up fighting like Sevareid and Port had at a similar point in theirs.

An hour later, as José heated his ramen breakfast in the bow, I leafed through *Canoeing with the Cree* until I found the passage:

Like children, we bickered.

And then we came to blows. One cold morning, as we prepared to load the canoe, a trifling incident occurred which now I cannot even remember. Something in our minds snapped, our moral strength broke down. We leaped at each other. Hitting and twisting violently as though we were fighting for our lives, we rolled over and over until we struck a tree trunk.

When the fighting stopped, Sevareid and Port quickly realized the foolishness of their antagonism, and the extent to which they needed one another. The same was true for José and me. In fact, we had needed each other for some time before the trip even began.

After three hours of relatively relaxed paddling, we approached a town named Aubigny. I reminded José what Constable James had said about the route between Letellier and Winnipeg. "Don't waste your time going to Aubigny," he'd advised. "It's further off the river than it seems, and there's nothing to the town."

José scrambled up the retaining rocks and onto the roadway. "At home I run my family, but out here you run me? Is that how you think it's gonna be?"

I tied the canoe to some tree roots and followed him, the silence heavy between us. He paused briefly in the center of Aubigny, which consisted of a few small houses and a grocery store long out of business. He walked to the store, rattled and kicked the locked doors, then snorted at me as he passed, headed back to the river.

MÉTIS DREAMS

The following day, we paddled some 30 miles, then stashed our gear under a bridge and tramped up into a little Francophone village called Ste. Agathe as the day's light faded. The only illuminated establishment in town was the Ste. Agathe Inn, an old-time lodging house that attracted us like moths. Inside we found a pool table, a projection TV, pig feet in jars, and a stunning bartender with full lips, bronze skin, and jet-black hair. Her name was Ashley, and she quickly became José's latest obsession.

Ashley told us she was Métis, a mix of Cree, Ojibwe, and French. Raised on an impoverished reservation in central Manitoba, where alcoholism and suicide were endemic, she had found this job and enrolled at the University of Manitoba, where she was pursuing a degree in international studies. She would soon graduate, and hoped to find a job with an NGO that built and administered refugee camps in Africa. After doing that for a few years, she planned to return to Manitoba and make a meaningful contribution to the community she was from.

Just as she was offering this idealistic vision, my phone

blew up. I took the call from Gemma outside, on the steps of the inn. She said in a very sad voice that everything was fine at home, and that her summer had been a lot of fun so far. I asked her to tell me what was bothering her, but she refused, likely mindful of the fact that bad news from home would make it harder for me to stay on the river.

Seven-year-old Malcolm took the phone next, displaying no such restraint. "Dad," he cried, "where are you?"

When I told him we were in Canada, he thought that meant I was coming home. I explained that we still had hundreds of miles to go, and that I'd come home as soon as I reached the ocean.

"You promised," he screamed. "Just come home now!"

I returned to the beverage room, choking on guilt and longing for my kids.

Ashley was perched on the edge of a pool table, rolling a tan cue against her thighs. José was seated on a chair at her knees.

Ashley noticed the change in my mood.

"Bad news?" she asked.

I sat next to her on the pool table. Her query initiated a lengthy conversation about family dynamics, children, and divorce, an exchange José continually interrupted. Ashley talked about her mother and how much she missed being home. I told her about my former marriage, and about my kids. As we talked, Ashley turned off the deep fryer, scraped the grill, and swept behind the bar. Before long she was turning the key in the lock on the front door.

As we said good night beneath a vintage streetlamp, Ashley mentioned that an Aboriginal Day powwow would take place the following day at the Forks in Winnipeg, a historic gathering place at the junction of the Red and Assiniboine Rivers. If we could paddle some 35 miles between now and then, perhaps we'd meet again there.

"We'll be there," promised José. "If the old man here is up to it!"

Back beneath the Ste. Agathe bridge, I wondered aloud how José was going to juggle two women—Ashley and Homegirl J—during the few days we planned to spend in Winnipeg. He was entirely unconcerned, and quickly fell asleep.

As José slept beside me in the tent, I studied a map of Winnipeg in the light of my headlamp. Sevareid and Port had stayed at the Winnipeg Canoe Club, a fraternal order of paddling enthusiasts, where they were offered a tent site, fellowship, and detailed information on the route ahead. My map showed a sizable parcel of green real estate nestled within a large U-shaped river bend just south of the city. It was still designated as the Winnipeg Canoe Club.

I opened *Canoeing with the Cree* and read Sevareid's account of the boys' stay.

We were taken right into the "family" of more than a thousand members. Sam Southern, the "skipper," we found to be very hospitable. Caretaker, canoe builder and repairer, as well as unofficial father of all troubles and fount of all wisdom about the place, he immediately took charge of us, fixed up our boat on a suitable rack and granted permission for us to camp beside the club. In another tent, alongside ours, was "Tim" Buffington, the Winnipeg movie censor, who seemed to take an interest in us and drove us to the downtown district on more than one occasion.

I imagined benefiting from comparable hospitality, but it seemed unlikely that Winnipeg still employed a movie censor.

In the morning I tracked down the phone number for the Canoe Club. My call was promptly answered. "Canoe Club, this is Jake."

I explained that we were paddling through and needed a place to camp and store our gear while we conducted business in the city.

Jake laughed. "We haven't been that kind of club in years! This is a country club, a golf course. We're only called the Canoe Club because we're located on the same property." He hastened to add, though, that he, too, was an avid canoeist. And he encouraged us to camp there, so long as we remained out of sight of the golfers. "If you need anything at all," Jake concluded kindly, "I'll be working all week in the pro shop."

Determined to meet Ashley at the powwow, José paddled that day like the Energizer Bunny on Red Bull, into 20-mile-per-hour winds on whitecapped straightaways that often stretched a mile or more into the distance before switching back. By early afternoon we had reached the Perimeter Highway bridge at the edge of the city, and shortly thereafter we recognized a heavily tagged, wood-paneled structure on the eastern bank. We had reached the Canoe Club.

In spite of the fact that Winnipeg is a relatively compact city, it would be several hours before the meandering waterway brought us to the Forks. I suggested we stop at the Canoe Club and consider camping there. José responded quickly and decisively. There was no way in hell he was stopping short of the powwow.

He shot a photo of the Canoe Club, an edifice covered in so much spray paint it would have fit on the South Side of Chicago. "There," he sneered. "Now you can tell everyone you've been to that nigga Sevareid's little clubhouse."

We pressed on, and as the white high-rises on the University of Manitoba campus poked above the horizon, I felt the exhilaration that came with reaching another prominent milestone on our journey.

It was time to touch base with our local contact, Renny Davis, an old friend from high school. Now living in Winnipeg, Renny had agreed to take delivery of the barrel of freeze-dried foods I'd sent ahead from Saint Paul.

José found my phone sealed safely in two waterproof bags, inside the waterproof food barrel. He reached across the Duluth packs and set it carefully in my palm, a protocol we'd followed religiously whenever valuables were transferred between bow and stern.

I found Renny's contact and went to press call, but before I could do so, an incoming call from the Saint Paul area code appeared on the screen. When I answered, one of José's aunties asked if she could speak with him. I handed the phone back across the packs, setting it in José's palm.

They talked for what seemed like an eternity. José expressed jubilation, then a troubling seriousness.

"Don't do anything until I give the word," he signed off. "I'll call back soon."

After ending the call, José paddled awkwardly, holding the cell phone between his palm and the paddle in his top hand. He said, "I have that Sonic motherfucker in my scope. Auntie Florida has this guy named Buck inside the Stillwater pen; she has something going on with him. Buck is a skinny Ojibwe dude, but he looks white and has blue eyes, so he has to be extra brutal to get respect as a Native on the inside. That's how he rose through the ranks while doing time for aggravated assault. They have a tribal structure among the Indians in Stillwater, and Buck is the war chief. That means he decides on any attacks made by Natives against other prisoners. If he tells another Native dude he has to shank someone, that dude has to carry it out, even if it's not his beef."

As luck would have it, Sonic had recently been sentenced to a year behind bars for dealing crack, and was now assigned to Buck's cellblock. Buck was burning to put a hit on him. Everything was set, according to Florida: on José's word, in a maximum-security prison hundreds of miles to the south, the war chief would flash a sign to a foot soldier across the yard, setting in motion a brutal attack on José's archenemy.

"What are you going to do?" I asked.

He emitted a growl. "Don't talk to me."

As we rounded another bend, the university campus came into full view. Remembering that I still needed to call Renny, I slid onto my knees to take the phone. Instead of following protocol, José turned back and tossed it in my direction. I stretched over the gunwale to catch the errant throw, but the phone merely grazed my fingertips before sinking to an unholy grave.

"Shit, dawg," José said. "I threw that right to you. You shoulda had that."

I stared into the hypnotic ripples, then looked up at José. Initially I had thought it a simple misstep. But when I took in his expression, it quickly dawned on me that he had intentionally discarded the phone, in order to avoid calling in the hit on Sonic.

José had apparently seen the whole picture long before it crystallized for me. He realized that if Sonic were attacked in Stillwater, retribution would await him when he returned to Saint Paul. On the other hand, if he declined to call in the hit, he would look like a bitch. The kid solved a difficult problem with a simple act. For the time being, however, our situation was that much more complicated.

I reflected on it as we paddled to shore in the midst of campus. We found our way to the student union and devoured a lunch of tacos and doughnuts. I found Renny's number in the directory dangling beneath the union's pay-phone, and left a message indicating that we were pushing out of the university and would paddle as far as the Forks, where we were planning to attend a powwow. I would try to call again in two hours, when I expected to arrive.

Four hours later, all of it spent paddling into a rip-ping headwind, we reached the mouth of the Assiniboine, turned west into the current, and found a vacant dock near open-air bars and restaurants packed with Winnipeggers celebrating the balmy evening. As I prepared to step out of the canoe, Renny suddenly appeared on the dock, looking just as I had remembered him.

Having correctly calculated wind and distance from the university to the Forks, Renny had arrived at the docks a few minutes before us. He'd known for weeks of our plans to paddle the 500 miles from the headwaters to his city, but apparently he never really believed it. He gazed down at us now in disbelief. "You guys are insane!" he shouted.

Renny invited us to spend the next few nights with him and his family. This was more than I had expected, but I also knew that José had his heart set on hanging out with Ashley. I didn't accept the offer immediately, but I couldn't stop thinking of all it entailed: showers, couches, laundry, and a safe place to store the canoe while we caroused about town and restocked our food stores for the remote miles to come.

We ripped the spray deck from its Velcro attachments

and exposed Renny to 17 days of Red River filth. Two inches of charcoal-colored slosh covered the canoe's bottom. In it floated brawny black flies and mosquitoes, swollen crackers and ramen noodles, cigarette butts and various rotting accrual.

After José and I tacitly agreed that we were accepting the generous offer, Renny and José loaded the gear onto their backs while I pulled the canoe to my knees and popped it onto my shoulders. A viscous stew splashed down, streaming across my face and down my legs.

We crossed a plaza between the children's museum and a nightclub, and pressed through a crowd surrounding a magician. The parking lot hummed with people leaving the powwow, and as we walked through I noticed several heartbreakingly beautiful women who could have been Ashley's sisters.

We strapped the canoe atop Renny's truck and drove west on Portage Avenue, along the Assiniboine River. As we passed shopping malls and fast-food strips, I began to crash. I felt claustrophobic and anxious, and fought against a knee-jerk desire to turn around and return to the river.

Seeing Renny dredged up long-buried memories from my adolescence. When I played on the varsity hockey team, he played with my younger brother. During my junior year I had dated his sister, Stephanie—a kind, pretty, and popular cheerleader whose parents offered me their basement when I ran away from home at 16.

As we pulled into Renny's driveway in the Charleswood neighborhood, his 7-year-old stepdaughter, Kerri, skipped out of the house sporting a merry toothless grin.

Renny's wife, Celeste, a demure 25-year-old with a flaxen ponytail, met us in the garage. Her eyes moved from our grimy gear, which was piled in the corner next to her daughter's Schwinn, to our grimy bodies. She gave Renny a sideways glance and asked how long we were planning to stay. When I said we were hoping for two or three days to regroup, her face betrayed displeasure.

Before entering Renny and Celeste's tidy domain, we removed most of our clothing in the backyard and sprayed each other down with a garden hose. Then José tiptoed into the house to take a proper shower and Renny helped me drag the rest of the gear into the yard, where we cleaved layers of hardened earth with high-pressure spray and hung it from the clothesline. After a sublime 20-minute shower of my own, I scrubbed stubborn silt from the bottom of the porcelain tub.

After Renny tucked Kerri in for the night, he ordered a pizza. José and I devoured it in our boxers and T-shirts while the rest of our clothing spun in the washer. Then Renny sat with us on the cool basement floor, and we all studied a road map of Manitoba.

My plan was to put the canoe back in the water at Norway House, a Cree community on the northern tip of Lake Winnipeg, about 300 miles due north. Unfortunately, there was no way to secure passage to Norway House by water, the train didn't go there, a flight would be too expensive, and the drive, much of it by dirt road, would cover some 500 miles. When I asked Renny if he'd be willing to drive us to Norway House, he responded with dismissive laughter.

When asked for input, José hit pause on his CD player and insisted he wasn't going "nowhere no how until we hit the clubs with Homegirl J."

"You said we'd have hos, bro," he whispered, respectful of Renny and the females in the house. "I'm gonna need a week or two to work it round here. Put out the word, papi's in town."

I spent the remainder of the evening taking inventory of our food on the basement floor. I listed what remained from the barrel we had traveled with to this point, then compared it to the list of items in the barrel I had sent ahead before departing Saint Paul.

I lay awake that night, unaccustomed to being indoors. After turning it over every which way, I decided just before drifting off that we would rent a car and drive to Norway House. I was determined to whisk José north before Homegirl J showed up.

After a few hours of good sleep, I awoke to what seemed like a bad dream: schoolchildren repeating patriotic verse to the tune of "Sing a Song of Sixpence." Standing on Renny's basement couch, I peered out the window. Across the lane stood a red-brick elementary school, and in its paved courtyard a regiment of fair children belted the anthem with what sounded like genuine enthusiasm.

We are all Canadians
Living in this land.
If you were a Canadian
You would understand
Why we love our country
And why we are so proud.

We are proud Canadians
And we will shout it loud!

Upstairs, I found a note from Celeste welcoming us to anything in the kitchen. I helped myself to donuts and orange juice, then used Renny's international long-distance line—a perk of his employment with an American telecommunications firm—to call my children. As I dialed, a series of lightning blasts raced from my shoulder to my brain, the result of 500 miles of river travel.

The news from home was both encouraging and heartbreaking. Gemma, who had been training and performing for several years with a youth circus school, said she'd received a letter welcoming her to audition for Cirque du Soleil. The world's most famous circus, which she'd long dreamed of joining, would be holding tryouts "in a nearby city" within a few months. Apparently the producers were impressed by a video of her performing on the Spanish web and flying trapeze. Her excitement was unmistakable, and I choked up as she spoke.

Malcolm was next on the line. His palpable sadness set off another volley of pains in my neck. Unable to hold the phone to my ear, I placed the handset on the kitchen table and talked into it, doing my best to comfort him. "We're going as fast as we can," I explained, and promised to be home before July 30, his sixth birthday.

José came upstairs just as Renny appeared in the kitchen, toting a coffee mug. José asked him for an iron. I looked at him, puzzled. "Gonna need to get my fit smooth for them hos, bros," he explained, touching up his hair in the oven's reflection.

Later that morning, the stylish college student at the rental car company, Brittany, didn't hesitate when José asked her where we would find the hottest club in town. "The Tijuana Yacht Club," she said. "It's a young, hip crowd, cheap drinks, lots of pretty girls, and great music. Is that what you have in mind?"

José nodded knowingly, then paid close attention as she sketched directions to the club on the back of the rental car agreement.

When I told her we would need the car for a few weeks but would be staying within the province, Brittany warned that there weren't three weeks of roadway in all of Manitoba. I explained my complex plan. We would drive to Norway House, where I would leave José with the canoe and gear. Then I would take the car 120 miles west on a dirt road to Wabowden, a tiny Cree village that was the nearest place to Norway House with both a passenger rail line and road access. I would park the car in Wabowden and take the Grey Goose bus back to Norway House, where we would put the canoe back in the water and continue with our journey to Hudson Bay. After a few weeks we would return to the rental car via floatplane and train, and drive it back to Winnipeg.

Brittany was ashen. "You intend to leave that brand-new 2006 Chevy Malibu in an Indian village for more than five minutes? And you expect that it will be there when you get back? Are you sure you want to decline the additional insurance?" The only possibility, she went on, would be to park near the RCMP station, where the police might keep an eye on it.

I scratched my initials on the "decline insurance" line, put off by Brittany's racist warning.

As we pulled out of the lot, José agreed. "At first I thought that broad was dope," he said, "then I thought she was just stupid." José didn't let this opinion affect the way he felt about the nightclub Brittany had recommended, however. At his insistence we drove around town until we located it.

The Tijuana Yacht Club made a sad impression beneath the bright afternoon sky. Its entrance was the nondescript side door of an AmericInn near the Polo Park shopping mall—the kind of door you'd walk through on the way to a grimy parking garage.

José remained optimistic. "Shit," he whistled. "There's gonna be hos."

After lunch I drove all the way up Portage Avenue to the Forks. It was happening again. The anxiety squatting inside me had awakened like a hungry baby from its nap, and was screaming bloody murder. José turned Kanye way up, grooving with his hands above his head, and rapping to bleach-blonde high school girls in a black Mustang at a stoplight. I turned the music down as we rolled along.

I parked at the Forks and walked to the dock where we

had disembarked the night before. I hiked past it and up the banks of the Assiniboine, my dry shoes sinking into the familiar mud while José followed. "Why the hell we back at the river?" he shouted. "I paddled my ass off to get here so we could forget the goddamn river." At the confluence I walked north a few minutes up the gunky banks, and breathed its breeze like medicine.

Stepping onto a sandbar to get a view upriver, I stared enviously at the vanishing point, remembering that while he and Port were furloughed in Winnipeg, Sevareid, too, was afflicted with the insidious drag of urban life.

We liked the city very much, in our two days there. The evenings we spent lolling near the club dock, watching the young men and women swim and paddle or play golf and tennis or dance, were unforgettable since everyone treated us like guests. But they were dangerous. Until now we had thought only of the great adventure we were on, but now we grew a trifle homesick for these soft pleasures of city life. Had we stayed there much longer, probably we might have given up.

I decided silently to leave the following day. If José were to have his action, it would have to happen that night.

Later that evening, we took our place in line outside the Tijuana Yacht Club. It took no time for José to select his object of obsession for the evening. The only Native girl in

the queue as far as we could tell, she was petite and curvaceous, a long-haired brunette with large doe eyes.

"Day-yam, hell yeah, oh, hell yeah, dawg. I'm funna hit
that," he sang in my ear, his eyes glued to the pretty girl's
backside.

José ditched me the second we were in the raging temple.
He had a game plan and there wasn't a roster spot for the
"old guy" on this team. For the next few hours I glimpsed
José sporadically when he emerged from the pulsing crowd,
perspiring from his dogged pursuit, asking me to buy him
drinks before wandering off again, increasingly inebriated.

I killed the night with a dozen trips to the bar, downing beers, tequila shots, and gin and tonics, numbing the
needling hurt that had spread from my neck into my heart.
Sometime after midnight, José appeared again to ask my
advice on how to approach his girl.

"She's out there dancing. I don't want to seem like I'm
trying to be sleazy. I can tell she's a respectable young lady."

"Just go out there and start dancing with her," I said. "If
she digs you she'll let you know. If she doesn't she'll ignore
you."

José wandered off, not to be seen again until 2:00 a.m.,
when he found me nearly passed out on a cushy couch behind the back bar. I could tell he was frustrated. I gave him
five bucks for another drink. He sipped it in shame, reporting that he'd finally worked up the courage to ask her to
dance. She declined, explaining that her feet hurt.

As we drove back to Renny's house, José repeated a

sloshed refrain: "Her feet hurt, bro. What kind of bullshit is that?"

José's hangover the next morning provided the perfect distraction for my escape plan. He rode along cooperatively as I drove from store to store, collecting foodstuffs and other goods for the rest of the journey.

We stopped at a pharmacy in Osborne Village to refresh our supply of Aleve, the over-the-counter anti-inflammatory that had been helpful in relieving the pinched nerves José and I suffered on the river. When I didn't find it on the shelf, I asked a pharmacist for help.

"You can't buy that in Canada without a prescription," she replied, before leading me to the shelf where I could buy "the closest thing to it." I don't recall the name of the drug she recommended, but I do remember the pharmacist suggesting that we not take them while paddling, explaining that they were "basically sleeping pills." I purchased two small bottles and added them to our first aid kit.

Our next stop was a day spa promising a special on pedicure and massage. José settled in for a nap in the front seat of the Malibu as I entered Soul Haven. It smelled of rose petals and camphor, and didn't strike me as the kind of place that was accustomed to serving men. The receptionist pushed her bifocals up her nose and half-heartedly perused the schedule for an available appointment. I explained my ragged appearance, describing the canoe journey so she would understand why I needed someone to pull the fork from my neck. She eventually dropped her airs, deciding she could squeeze me in with Janelle for half an hour.

I disrobed and crawled under a blanket on the massage table. Janelle came in wearing a beige dress uniform, buttoned up and pressed. I recall saying nothing untoward in describing my pain, but after asking about my needs, Janelle made clear, in a chastising tone, that this would be "just a relaxation massage." She stood three feet away until I assured her that I understood. I expected a temporary reduction in pain, not a happy ending.

Miraculously, Janelle healed me. I fell asleep, and when I awoke 20 minutes later the agony in my neck was gone.

José's mood turned salty that afternoon. As we walked among the hundreds of colorful bins at the Scoop & Save, a bulk-food grocer we were lucky to stumble upon as we roamed the city, he seemed inexplicably furious about my visit to "that place for old broads."

I jammed a scoop into the Spanish peanuts and asked him to drop it. I'd been in extreme pain and now I felt better. What was the big fucking deal?

"You've gone soft, Lurie," he replied.

I threw down the scoop and asked what the hell his problem was.

He got in my face and demanded to know why I needed "a pedi or whatever the fuck" to make my back feel better for a canoe trip. He obviously thought I'd gone in and had my toes done. When I explained what had happened, José realized his error, rubbed his forehead, and slumped off to ponder the jawbreakers.

For the remainder of the journey we would subsist on freeze-dried food and trail mix. Since I had sent the former ahead to Renny, now I filled triple-lined plastic bags with pretzels, dried cereal and fruit, nuts and seeds. It was hard to gauge how much we would need for what was likely to be a monthlong paddle.

Back in the Malibu, we inched through rush hour traffic, finally arriving in Renny's suburb just as a call came in from Homegirl J.

José was uncharacteristically hushed as he listened, mumbling every few minutes. "Oh really. I see how it is. Yeah, it's a pretty boring drive. I don't know how long until I'm back in Frogtown."

"That's it for that bitch," José said after ending the call. "That lazy ho was on her way here, but an hour out of Saint Paul she got bored and turned around. That's how it is. The bitch got bored," he mocked, trying to disguise his disappointment.

When we arrived at Renny's we found him at the back-yard grill, forming a pile of white powdery briquettes. Burgers sat on a plate covered with tinfoil. His head hung as we greeted him, like a father disappointed with irresponsible sons. We had arrived 30 minutes late for dinner.

The house smelled of corn on the cob and melted margarine, and the table in Renny's dining room was set with placemats and matching glassware. Celeste worked up a

smile and asked us to wash our hands and sit down. Renny
nodded at Kerri as she said grace.

Celeste's feeling for José was striking. She mothered
him lovingly over dinner, spooning boiled potatoes onto
his plate from steaming Corningware. She stabbed him a
sausage and offered that there were plenty more. She kindly
pointed out a piece of sage stuffing on the corner of his lips.
She asked him about his parents, his siblings, and what he
wanted to do with his life.

José answered tersely and with more than a hint of embarrassment, as if there was something terrible in his past. I
remember distinctly how he talked about his mother: "She
meant well, but she wasn't right in the head. My big brother
was in prison half my childhood, and I was the one who
took care of the other kids. My mom used to make us stay
in our rooms for hours, while she was drinking and smoking crack with her boyfriends."

Celeste's maternal attention and gentle inquisitive-
ness seemed to nourish José. He let his shoulders down,
melted into his high-backed chair, and went on. "I would
sneak out of my room searching for packs of ramen. We
would sprinkle on the flavor packets and chew on the dry
noodles. One time my big brother and I came out of the
room because my mom was getting beat up by one of her
boyfriends. I broke a liquor bottle over his head and then
mopped up the blood while we waited for the police and
ambulance."

Renny looked increasingly uneasy as he went on, but

José was clearly enjoying the attention. His face shone. "When the cops got there I told them it was self-defense. But they still cuffed me and made me sit out on the curb for a long time in the middle of the night."

Celeste nodded and murmured in a way that seemed to unburden José's spirit. I was heartened to see him finally getting the kind of female attention he needed.

After coffee and chocolate cake, Renny helped us load our packs and food barrels into the trunk of the Malibu, and fasten the canoe to its roof. José shook Renny's hand, said goodbye to Kerri, and offered his hand to Celeste. She ignored it, wrapped her arms around his shoulders and held him long enough for the awkward uncertainty to melt from his face, replaced by a crimson flush. She made him promise to be careful. As we backed out of the driveway, Renny and Celeste stood together with their arms intertwined, waving as if they were sending sons off to war.

As I accelerated onto Portage Avenue, we passed dozens of bars, and the Tijuana Yacht Club. We merged onto Highway 6, the blacktopped artery that runs between the mammoth Lakes Winnipeg, Manitoba, and Winnipegosis. Soon the city lights dissipated in my rearview mirror and we were plunged into the moonless darkness through which we would drive until sunrise.

ON TO NITASKINAN

José snoozed in his sleeping bag while I guided the Malibu beneath the Milky Way. In the enveloping blackness of the Interlake region—the strip of land between Lake Winnipeg and Lake Winnipegosis—I felt as if the car were pulling the tendrils of mist blasting the windshield toward us, like space dust to gravity. Every 30 or 40 kilometers, brilliant petrol signs pierced the firmament, indicating the proximity of postage-stamp population centers such as Lake Francis, Oak Point, Camper, Deerhorn, Moosehorn, and Grand Rapids. Beyond the reach of radio transmissions, I drove through the night in silence, my thoughts on Lake Winnipeg, the inland sea that paralleled the route to our east.

Around midnight, somewhere south of Oak Point, I steered onto the abandoned shoulder of Highway 6 and stepped out onto the tarmac. Exhausted and exhilarated, I sat against the rear bumper in the starlight, thumbing through my well-worn copy of *Canoeing with the Cree*. I quickly located the passage in which Sevareid conveys his first impression of Lake Winnipeg: "My feeling was one of immediate emptiness in the pit of the stomach."

Some 50 miles north of the city of Winnipeg, the Red River empties into the big lake, which presented Sevareid and Port with new challenges.

Oh, there was a difference in lake paddling! And there was a science to it. We learned fast—we had to.

On our second jump, to Balsam Bay, the waves began coming in from the side and as minutes went by they gained in size. Taken at the wrong moment, we were apt to receive the white crest of the breaker right over our packs and our legs. Our paddling had to be carefully timed and we had to sit lightly in the boat, relaxed at the hips, and allow it to roll all it pleased. That is the secret of successful rough-water canoeing.

After several close calls, including one time when a screaming roller nearly smashed them onto the rocky shore, Sevareid and Port adapted to paddling on Lake Winnipeg. But as they gained command of their canoe, a new fear arose: Indians. Seventy years later, I couldn't help but smile at the recognition that their attitude toward Indians bore some resemblance to José's take on white people. They also had a similar reaction to that fear, opting to sleep beside a gun and an ax. "For exactly what use they would be employed we were not quite sure," Sevareid wrote, "but we had vague imaginings, acquired from books and stories."

When Sevareid and Port initially encountered indigenous people, instinct took over. Banished to the rocky shore of Black Island by stiff winds one afternoon, they spotted a canoe on the water. "Troubled about their intentions," recounted Sevareid, "we slid our canoe into the brush and lay waiting out of sight." As they passed, he observed a boat "laden with Indian children. An old squaw, seated cross-legged in the stern, steered with a paddle."

Back on the road after a short break, José slumbered in the passenger seat. I stopped for gas at a truck stop in St. Martin's Junction. As I sat on the hood and sipped a cup of coffee, I scanned my copy of *Canoeing with the Cree*, wondering at the fact that none of the commentaries I'd read on Sevareid's narrative had criticized his representation of Natives. The paperback edition in my hands had been reissued to commemorate the 75th anniversary of the expedition, and included a forward by Arctic explorer Ann Bancroft. A minor celebrity in Minnesota, Bancroft and I had some things in common: we had both lived in Ely (a small town in northern Minnesota), we had both spent significant periods of time on the same Lakota reservations in South Dakota, and we knew some of the same people. Her father, Dick Bancroft, whom I'd met while covering a story in Pine Ridge, South Dakota, had made a name for himself in the seventies as the photodocumentarian of the American Indian Movement. And now, rereading the foreword, I noticed that Ann Bancroft had developed "a love for canoes" while paddling out of Widjiwagan, the sister camp to Menogyn, where I'd spent five summers paddling the Boundary Waters Canoe Area Wilderness, as well as the lakes and rivers of Ontario. But it was the romanticism inherent in the one mention of Indians in the foreword that caught my attention now: "Readers can imagine the hushed sounds of the native Cree language, the feel of rabbit-fur moccasin liners, the scent of native white pine forests, and the distant whistle of 'iron' foreshadowing a noisier, more time-pressed day."

I was chagrined. For the Cree of northern Manitoba, Sevareid and Port weren't simply a pair of chums on what Bancroft described as "a fantastic adventure." They were harbingers of the wholesale destruction of Cree lands and culture, a process that began in earnest within a decade of the publication of this account of the boys' grand adventure.

While I spun the tires in the gravel at the edge of the highway, José sat up and blinked at the glow from the gas station. "Yo," he yawned. "What up, nigga? Where we at?"

I told him we were roughly halfway up the shore of Lake Winnipeg.

"Oh, hell no, bro," he replied. "That's one big fucking lake."

My headlights illuminated the eyes of several deer grazing in the ditches. I eased off the gas and pointed them out to José, but he had resumed snoring.

Every hour or so, I pulled off Highway 6 and spent a few minutes reading Sevareid to keep from falling asleep at the wheel. He and Port took a week to paddle from the Winnipeg Canoe Club to Berens River, a roadless First Nations reserve on the opposite shore from where José and

I were traveling. They wandered among the "mud-caulked cabins in which the Crees lived," stopped and chatted with "several old, lined squaws," and eventually stumbled upon "Chief Berens himself."

Sevareid expressed disappointment upon meeting this "ruler of some 300 Crees." He had expected to find the chief "in his wigwam, surrounded by his squaw and papooses, involved in consultation with his medicine men." Rather, Sevareid reported,

> He was reclining in a most undignified position in a frayed and dirty hammock, under a tree in his front yard, smoking, not a peace pipe, but a foul, black instrument that moved about between his lips as though it had been there for years and years—and it had.

What Sevareid referred to as a "peace pipe" is known among the Lakota (who were originally gifted the pipe from the White Buffalo Calf Woman) as a *canunpa*, or sacred pipe. The *canunpa* is used for prayer and ceremony, not for casual smoking.

A north wind and foul weather kept the boys in Berens River for several days. They passed much of this time with a city girl from Winnipeg named Betty Kemp, who seemed to take a liking to Port. After the three spent "delightful hours" dangling their "bare legs from a smooth shelf of granite into the cool waters," and "munching handfuls of rich, fat sand cherries," Port and Betty broke away from Sevareid for late-night swims.

Sevareid had plenty of time to observe the Berens River community. In 1925, the Cree were living between two worlds, still tied to traditional ways but also increasingly connected to the modern industrial world. The combination caught Sevareid's attention, if not always in ways that seem perceptive in retrospect. He noted, for example, that the Cree girls "wore their clothing with a stiff erectness; their skirts and blouses were ill-fitting and, indeed, all the beauty that should have been theirs was spoiled." Unmentioned, however, is the fact that Native children were often taken from their families and sent to distant boarding schools, where they were forced to dress and act like white people. They were severely punished for speaking their languages, and often prevented from seeing their families. It seems reasonable to assume that the young people Sevareid encountered were among the lucky ones who were permitted to spend that summer with their families.

Sevareid's disapproval of the Indians contrasted with his gushing admiration for the "young white men that rule the north." He described the crew of the Berens River forestry station as a "splendid bunch. All of them young and strong and intelligent." To the boys' credit, however, they recognized racist attitudes in other outsiders after a few days in Berens River. When a group of white tourists disembarked from a steamer, Sevareid was upset by the way they gathered around Chief Berens and "asked him silly questions like, 'Do you have any papooses?' Some of them actually held out pieces of candy, as though he were a bear in a zoo."

After waiting three days for the northerlies to subside, Sevareid and Port decided to leave Berens River. It was late August, and with more than 600 river miles between them and Hudson Bay, the boys were running out of time. In fact, when Sevareid was warned in Berens River that it would be suicide for them to continue into the wilderness with winter fast approaching, the boys heeded the admonition and agreed to wait two days for the steamer *Wolverine*, which took them overnight to Norway House.

Minutes before sunrise, the horizon took on the faint hue of cherry. Exhausted, I swerved off the highway and parked on the shoulder of a power-line road. When we awoke not long after dawn, black flies orbited our heads. They were furry and muscular and seemingly everywhere.

José started from his slumber and screamed: "Oh, hell no, bro, drive, drive, drive!"

I accelerated and opened all four power windows.

"What are you doing?" José panicked. "Close the windows, they'll get in!"

"They're already in," I snorted, "we have to let them out!"

"Fuck! Fuck!" he shouted, swatting in vain.

A mile up the road, only a dozen or so of them remained, perched on the rear window and licking their feet, planning their next attack. I prayed that the flies were a local phenomenon. I'd been on several canoe trips punctuated by their excruciating bites, and knew that paddling the next

500 miles with a flying escort would turn what promised to be an extreme challenge into a bloody death march. Alas, when we slowed at a gas station in Grand Rapids, a Cree village located at the mouth of the Saskatchewan River on the northwestern banks of Lake Winnipeg, the hordes descended again on the Malibu.

José had many needs that morning. He was hungry and thirsty, and he had to use the bathroom. But when he saw the blitzkrieg he refused to leave the safety of our mobile bomb shelter.

I hesitated too, watching to see how the Native people—coming and going from the convenience store, filling their gas tanks, bending over to tie a shoe—coped with the threat. But I was amazed to observe them going about their business as if there were no flies at all.

José noticed my hand moving to the door handle. "Close that shit quick," he commanded. "Don't let them bitches in here! What the fuck they feeding these flies anyways?"

I breathed cautiously as I filled the tank. In the tense calm of the moment, I noticed that while the flies whizzed and buzzed around me with intimidating ferocity, I had not yet been bitten. In fact, not a single fly had so much as alighted upon my skin.

When I walked into the convenience store I was engulfed by the aroma of fried foods: chicken fingers, potato wedges, cheese sticks, all warmed in paper trays under red lamps. A Grey Goose bus schedule was posted on the wall beside an antismoking advertisement featuring full-color images of some poor Canadian's malignant lungs. I checked the clock above the cashier's stand—it was June 22, 7:00 a.m.—then ran my finger down the timetable to the Wabowden stop. The motor coach would stop here later that day, en route to Norway House.

I was overwhelmed with a sense of urgency. If I was going to get us situated for the next phase of the journey, we would have to drop José, the canoe, and all our gear in Norway House—290 miles away—by two o'clock in the afternoon. If I missed that bus, it would be three days before the next one.

I bought two Cokes and two bags of ranch-flavored Doritos, and tossed the snacks onto the sleeping bag covering José's lap. "Breakfast Frogtown style," he declared happily.

As we merged back onto the highway, José began devouring the Doritos, then made it clear that he would never leave the car again.

"How will we paddle to Hudson Bay if you won't go outside?" I asked.

"We won't, bro," he replied, his voice devoid of the comical lilt upon which his words often glided. And then, more ominously: "Trip's over unless the flies disappear."

An hour down the dirt roadway stretching from the Highway 6 turnoff to Norway House, thick pine forest gave way to a wide blue sky. I pulled to a stop on a gravel ridge above an angry Lake Winnipeg. Ahead, a long white structure, which I recognized as the Jenpeg dam, spanned the quarter-mile width of the Nelson River. I parked the car but left it running so José, sleeping again, wouldn't get chilled.

Outside, the north wind screamed across open water, an arctic blast that smelled of pine sap and stung like ice. On the upstream side of the dam, cobalt waters strained against confinement, leaping and foaming as far as the eye could see. Gazing out at the reservoir through the jumble of transformers and high-tension wires of the Jenpeg power station, I was overcome with a sense of outrage.

I had thought of this place many times since reading a transcript of a speech given by Chief John Miswagon, leader of the Pimicikamak Cree Nation, at the University of St. Thomas on April 15, 2000. Miswagon had been in Saint Paul to make its residents aware that the source of the energy fueling their lifestyle was destroying Cree lands. At the time, 11 percent of the electricity consumed in the Twin Cities metropolitan area was generated by Manitoba Hydro's Nelson River dams.

I discovered the speech a few weeks after it was delivered, in some punk rock zine I'd picked up in a coffee shop in Anchorage. I fetched it from a sealed bag now, and returned to Miswagon's words as I looked down on the Jenpeg dam.

We Pimicikamak Crees are water and forest people who have lived in Nitaskinan—"Our Land"—for thousands of years. This remote subarctic habitat provides nesting and staging areas for the migratory species that use the Mississippi Flyway. And our boreal forests are absolutely essential to the health of this hemisphere.

Cross Lake, where we live, is 10 miles from the control gate that holds back the water in Lake Winnipeg and releases it into the Nelson River to generate power. The Nelson River drainage area stretches from Alberta in the west to Lake Superior in the east, to Hudson Bay in the north. It covers parts of Montana, North and South Dakota, Minnesota and your Boundary Waters Canoe Area.

When Manitoba Hydro arrived in Nitaskinan more than 30 years ago, it did not inform us of its plans. Nor were we asked for our consent. No comprehensive environmental assessments were conducted, no cultural inventories were taken.

To this day, we do not know how many species have been lost, how many habitats destroyed, or how many of our traditional campsites and burial grounds lie underwater, or disappeared during construction. We do know that we have lost burial sites, the entire fisheries of whitefish and sturgeon, our ability to travel safely on the waterways, and much of our ability to sustain ourselves on the land.

The impacts of your electricity use are invisible to you, although we are only 20 hours away by car.

The photographs projected behind me show the environmental wasteland near where we live. Because of unnatural fluctuations and water flows, islands and boreal forest shorelines are eroded and collapsing.

Across the world, indigenous peoples speak about their connection to the land. It is no different for us in the north. What looks like remote wilderness on a map to you is as familiar to us as the backs of our hands. Every stream, every hill, every marsh has a Cree name and a Cree history.

The builders of large hydroelectric projects use words like "self-renewing power," "green energy," and "safe electricity." But imagine the pain of a mother who must teach her children dirty words like *emach-akamik*, which refers to water polluted by the soil that washes into our water from the continual erosion of the river banks, and to water polluted by methyl mercury, which poisons the fish and animals.

Our community has very high rates of suicide and suicide attempts. Manitoba Hydro will tell you that there is no connection between its project and the poverty and despair existing in every affected Cree community, but the truth is that these projects are our nightmare.

I thought of Chief Miswagon's speech over the remainder of the morning drive, until we arrived in Norway

House, at the northern tip of Lake Winnipeg. The 5000 or so residents of the drowsy village lived in small homes, many of them with short docks and outboard fishing boats, nestled along the shores of Playgreen Lake, which constitutes the northern outlet of Lake Winnipeg and the headwaters of the Nelson River.

"This is the same Red River we paddled," I explained to José, extending the map across to the passenger seat. "But up here they call it the Nelson."

José pondered this without responding. He had never shown much interest in our route.

I went on. "The Red River empties into Lake Winnipeg, and eventually comes out here. This is the same river." He nodded, but still seemed uninterested.

The reception desk at the York Boat Hotel looked to be unattended, but we soon found a woman slumbering on a couch in the lobby. Long black hair masked her face, and the haphazard way she hung off the sofa led me to suspect that she had stumbled into the hotel in order to snore off a nasty binge.

José rapped his knuckles on the reception desk, "Yo, can we get a room?" He amplified his voice the way he did when he had identified a woman he wanted to impress.

We heard the squeak of a housekeeping cart, then spotted a maid pushing her towel-topped burden from the end of a long hallway. When she finally arrived she pointed at the couch, and backed her cart into the laundry room.

Feeling eyes upon her, the woman stirred and sat up. She

tripped across the lobby and through a door marked "Employees Only." She steadied herself against the cash register and explained that it was $65 for a double room.

When I looked into the woman's eyes it was immediately clear that she was not an elderly transient, as I had assumed initially, but rather a teenage girl. She apologized for "sleeping on the job," adding that she'd been at a graduation party until 5:00 a.m.

Noticing the canoe on the Malibu, she asked about our journey. When we explained what we were up to, she invited us to the party, which was set to resume that afternoon in a community hall behind the hotel. Then she picked up the phone and dialed the "chief." He would likely comp our hotel stay, she said, when he heard that "a Native guy from the States had stopped here on the way to Hudson Bay." The way she put this seemed to suggest that the 500-mile waterway from Norway House to Hudson Bay was a special route for the Cree.

The chief's secretary answered. The receptionist listened carefully, then turned back to us. "Unfortunately," she said, "he's out of the territory, at a conference down south. And he's the only person who can authorize the room charges." She suggested we notify the chief in advance the next time we were planning a trip to Norway House.

José was flabbergasted. "You serious? This is the first time being an Indian worked in my favor!"

As we unloaded the gear into our room, and set the canoe against the wall outside our window, I encouraged José to attend the party while I drove to Wabowden. After all, I explained, this would likely be his best opportunity to meet girls in Norway House.

I left José with $20 and drove like mad, back over the same dusty reserve road that had delivered us to Norway House. Once arrived in Wabowden, I hurried into the tiny Cree village's discount store and walked up to the counter. The thirtysomething cashier had the sad face of a chronic drinker, and the empathetic eyes of someone who has lived through hell. I trusted her instantly.

She sold me a ticket for the Grey Goose, which was set to depart the Wabowden Lucky Dollar for Norway House in 10 minutes. In a panic, I asked her where I could park the Malibu for a few weeks. I wondered aloud about the RCMP station I'd seen at the edge of town.

"You ain't gonna wanna park it there," the woman whispered. "Our people will go after it if they think it belongs to the police."

She tensed and dropped her eyes at the appearance of a short white man wearing an apron and an irate expression. When he slid behind her and reached for a clipboard, it became apparent that this was the store manager.

The woman, whose name tag read Edna, handed me the bus ticket and change, then thanked me for shopping at the Lucky Dollar.

He admonished her sharply. "Speak up when talking to the customers."

"Could you even hear her?" the manager asked in a bigoted

tone that was familiar to me from the years I had lived in Native communities.

"Yes." I smiled. "I can hear her perfectly."

I walked away from the checkout and browsed the aisles—dusty rows of overpriced canned goods, cheap plastic toys, snack cakes, and candies—waiting for the manager to leave. I selected a bottle of water and a chocolate bar for the ride to Norway House.

"The safest place to leave your car," Edna continued, "is in the yard outside my trailer. I've had troubles with my ex-husband, so I got Killer. Everyone around here is scared of my pit bull. No one messes with me anymore."

I found the trailer about three blocks from the Lucky Dollar, behind a mountain of gravel. Its windows were boarded with plywood and brown paint curled from the exterior, revealing patches of aluminum that reflected the afternoon sun. Had it not been for the beast snarling and straining against a thick chain by the front door, I would have assumed that the trailer was abandoned.

"It's alright, Killer," I said gently.

The pit bull bared his teeth.

I locked the Malibu and stood behind it, considering for a moment the potential consequences of leaving a rental car here, less than three body lengths from Edna's snarling dog. Not seeing a better alternative, I departed the yard cautiously, giving Killer wide berth.

I ran back up the hill as the Grey Goose coach pulled in front of the Lucky Dollar, shedding dust from the road.

I fished a $20 bill from my wallet to give to Edna. As I reached across the counter, she hesitated, then awkwardly handed me a copy of the *Winnipeg Free Press*. "Thank you, sir," she said, opening the cash drawer and slipping the money into the pocket of her smock. She pulled a discarded receipt from the top of an overflowing trash can, scribbled on the blank side, and handed it to me, smiling shyly.

As I took the note, I noticed for the first time Edna's natural beauty, and the irises of her burnt sienna eyes.

"What are you, Edna, some kind of famous celebrity?" The mean little manager appeared like the calvary from behind a shelf of snack cakes. "So you're a superstar now, giving autographs to the paparazzi?"

I silently thanked Edna and walked out to the Grey Goose. I shuffled to the back of the bus and found an empty seat among a handful of Cree teenagers. They regarded me with mild surprise, but were clearly more interested in the beats seeping from their iPods. I fell into a seat and pulled the furrowed receipt from my pocket.

"You seem nice," it read. "Look me up when you get back. XOXO, Edna."

THE HARBORMASTER

Upon my return to the York Boat Hotel, José reported that he had met a "dope-ass Cree broad" who worked at Chester's Fried Chicken. After she had served him the dark meat combo, José apparently returned several times over the course of her long shift, asking first for ice water, then for more ketchup and a little more honey for his biscuit. Finally, he asked where a man like himself, a Lakota from America, could buy a pack of cigarettes and a cold beer in this town?

While I drifted in and out of consciousness later that night, José paced the hotel room, debating internally whether he should go to the graduation party that raged through the darkness a few hundred yards from the hotel window. As an outsider, he felt insecure about joining the celebration. Or as he put it to me the following morning, "What would they say when some Mexican crashes their fiesta?" In the end, this social anxiety won out.

The northern sky over Norway House ignited at 4:30 the following morning. Not long after, José took a deep sniff, heaved a 75-pound pack onto his back, and tripped out onto the road with sleepy resignation. We began to walk the mile or so from the front door of the York Boat Hotel to Playgreen Lake. Surrounded by a magnificent wetland, the lake was golden and luminous under slanted beams of sun that torched the edges of wicked clouds. The day felt dangerous—beautiful and deadly. After a few steps, José stopped and turned to face me. "Which way, dawg?"

I made a command decision: José needed coffee.

We dropped our gear on a bench at the entrance to the hotel and walked across a vacant lot to a restaurant. We took a booth, and as I sat down across from José it occurred to me with sudden clarity that he was devastated by the disappointing outcome with the girl from Chester's.

I tried to buoy his spirits by pointing out all the characters in the restaurant, trying to get him to laugh. There was the local priest in his black slacks and collar; the tribal treasurer with his cowboy hat, bolo tie, boots, and fancy jacket; the preppy young Mormon missionary from down south with his tie and elder's nametag; and a table of chatty middle-aged Cree women speaking their native language. José looked around glumly.

As we walked back to the hotel, another idea came to mind. Perhaps I could improve José's disposition if I showed him some magic. I told him to leave the packs on the bench. They were loaded with our renewed food supply, and portaging them would have required doubling back for a second load. José initially appeared to be annoyed by my hesitation.

When I explained that the quickest way to get all our gear to the water would be to set the canoe by the hotel entrance and wait, he looked genuinely puzzled.

I've found people in Native communities to be generally curious about, and generous toward, outsiders. Having observed a segment of Norway House's population eating ham and eggs, I was certain this community was no different. No more than a minute after I told José that someone would offer us a ride to the boat landing, a Toyota pickup stopped on the street in front of us

"You guys look like you could use a ride!" said the driver, a cheerful, light-complexioned woman who looked to be in her forties.

We loaded the packs and barrels onto the short bed, then set my life jacket on top of the cab in order to protect the finish from the canoe. I glanced at José as we stood in the bed, steadying the canoe, surfing the smooth road as we rolled down to the water. His eyes were wide, as if he'd just witnessed a miracle.

As the driver brought us down to the harbor, José and I chatted with her through the moonroof. She introduced herself as "Marilyn York, like the boats." Since arriving in Norway House I'd noticed repeated references to York boats in the names of businesses, streets, and surnames. I surmised that there was some connection with York Factory, our destination on Hudson Bay.

The York boat, Marilyn explained, was the primary vehicle with which Europeans had settled central Canada. "They were to Canada what the covered wagon was to America. Whole families, desperate people from places like Scotland and Ireland, came off the big sailing ships at York Factory and loaded onto York boats, which were constructed on site by the Hudson's Bay Company."

The York boat, she went on, was fashioned after the Viking longship, and was so heavy it couldn't be portaged; it had to be rolled across trails on logs. "Imagine how difficult those poor people's journey to the interior must have been," she said, "rowing hundreds of miles against the Hayes River current, pushing those weighted-down boats up rapids and rolling them around waterfalls, all the way to Winnipeg."

As Marilyn continued, she grew increasingly animated. "The people of Norway House are descended from Indians and immigrants, for whom the York boat is a cultural symbol. And the sacred Hayes River route you are about to follow is still traveled by Crees in York boats."

As we came over a rise, the frothing turbulence of Playgreen Lake spread before us. An angry wind smacked my cheeks and lifted the canoe momentarily off the cab. Had Marilyn not pulled to a stop at the edge of an ivory beach, the canoe would have blasted off. The sight of the untamed waters held me transfixed. I felt untethered and exposed.

Before we knew what was happening, Marilyn heaved the canoe onto her shoulders and marched to where the waves slid across fine sands. After three quick trips, she had lugged nearly all the gear to the shore. In the meantime, I struggled to overcome the crippling realization that José and I were about to set out on angry water, alone again, through hundreds of miles of wilderness.

As soon as Marilyn departed—"late for work," she explained—we were approached by a portly Cree gentleman who paused to look over our gear, then identified himself as the harbormaster. His stern demeanor made me wonder what we had done wrong. He told us to follow him, and led us to a nearby shack on a spit of land at the base of a long pier.

We walked through a fenced courtyard and a web of picnic tables. A menu scribbled with black marker on the back of a pizza box was duct-taped to a post. It offered popsicles, hot dogs, pop, giant freezies, ice cream Drumsticks, and bottled water. Inside, the shack provided a cozy shelter from the tempest screaming off the lake. José and I sat on a loveseat with upholstered pillows, surrounded by candles, vases filled with fresh wildflowers, gnarled pieces of driftwood, and family photos.

Initially José was silent while I interacted with the harbormaster. He was used to acting hard around the Indians he knew back home, and he was probably intimidated. He may have felt, as I did, that we were in some trouble for not having obtained permission to shove off from reserve territory. It soon became clear, however, that the harbormaster was simply being gracious and hospitable.

"My kids are all grown and off to the cities," he said, noting how I took in a photo of him and several young ones, standing on the very beach where the canoe now awaited the next phase of our journey. "Don't ask about their mother, I haven't seen her in years. Just as well. I've never been happier." I envied the apparent freedom and simplicity of his existence.

As we chatted, the increasingly relaxed harbormaster intuited my questions. He said he made a modest living running the "sidewalk café," and explained his business model: "I buy a pallet of waters in Winnipeg for $10, and resell it here for $50."

The cafe was closed over the long winter, he went on, but over the course of the summer he usually sold things here and there, mostly to kids coming by on bikes. But he made his year during Treaty and York Boat Days, a weeklong annual gathering that drew thousands of participants and spectators to the annual powwow and York boat races. He invited us to return in early August, when the community would celebrate the event's 33rd anniversary.

He excused himself while he phoned the "Boss," who was, according to the harbormaster, "a fellow boater who would like to meet this Indian paddler from America who had come to retrace our route." José and I followed him outside to wait.

The harbormaster looked down the pier and laughed as if he'd pulled one over on us. "Keeping those secure," he said, pointing to a fleet of four large, open-faced boats tied to the end of the pier, "that's my real job. Those are professional racing York boats; they're made of aluminum, worth about $50,000 each. They used to use the old wooden boats, but they cost a fortune to maintain." The slick Yorks were painted like NASCAR bodies, with the names of sponsors—among them, Manitoba Hydro—emblazoned on the sides.

"It used to be just the people from here who raced," he went on, "but now they're coming in from other Cree communities—Oxford House, Cross Lake, Fisher River, Split Lake. Guys train all summer for a shot at the prize money. It's grueling work manning those 17-foot oars. Some of them they have arms like this." He indicated a space above his bicep the size of a football.

As if on cue, a young man with a long braid and massive arms entered the courtyard with what looked to be his wife and infant daughter. They were introduced by the harbormaster as the Boss and his family, though the man had to be 20 years younger than the harbormaster, and not much older than José.

As the cloudy day warmed into the sixties, a stiff wind kept the flies away. We sat at the harbormaster's picnic tables, and the Boss turned his attention to José, who was shy until asked where he was from.

José beamed proudly and explained that he was a Sicangu Lakota of the Oceti Sakowin, the Great Sioux Nation—"the people," he added, "who killed Custer at Little Bighorn." José never seemed to grasp how funny this proclamation sounded, but our new friends cracked up in response.

Noticing José's earnestness, the Boss quickly wiped the

smile off his face. "Oh yeah," he deadpanned, "the Sioux. I've heard of you guys."

Laughter was the only encouragement José needed in order to come out of his shell. He was obviously delighted not to have to prove himself to the Cree the way he did with his own people. He told them about his family's heritage, how his ancestors had been expelled from Minnesota during the state's genocidal campaign of 1862, and how they came to live among the Rosebud Lakota in South Dakota. He went on to explain that his family had moved to Chicago during the relocation period of the 1970s, but that gang violence in the city had eventually sent them packing again, back to Minnesota.

After a while the Boss said he needed to get back to work. We said goodbye to him and the harbormaster, thanking the older man for his hospitality and expressing our genuine desire to return one day for the York boat races. I couldn't help but envy him. If only I could live in a warm shack with a magnificent view, I thought, surrounded by a caring community, there would never again be cause for sadness.

The Boss and his family stood on the beach and watched as we loaded the canoe. Waves pounded the shore, and as we pushed the boat out into waist-deep water, they broke over the gunwales. José wrestled unwieldy packs into the surging boat. When there was nothing left on shore but two paddles, the Boss picked them up and walked into the waves, soaking his leather work boots and jeans. He handed me my paddle and nodded in a gesture of farewell. He did the same with José, then paused, placed a gentle hand on his shoulder, and said, "Thank you for what you're doing, young man. I'm proud of you. You're doing a really good thing."

The Boss held the canoe for us as we climbed over the gunwales. Powerfully moved by his gesture, I drove my paddle into the churning waters with tears streaming down my cheeks. With one simple gesture, José had finally received the acknowledgment from a Native man he had craved for so long.

"That was dope," José said as we pulled out onto deeper water. "That was so dope." He shook his head and leaned into his paddle with unprecedented determination.

There was no time to wallow in sentiment, however. We needed to focus on the challenge at hand or this new phase of the journey would end with us battered against the shore. Beyond the confines of a river channel for the first time, we would now be required to negotiate tricky winds and aggressive waves.

It quickly became apparent that I was leading us in the wrong direction. I looked back when I heard the Boss shouting through the growling wind. "Echimamish," he called, pointing northward down the jagged shoreline, toward the stream that runs between Playgreen Lake and the Hayes River.

I back-paddled, swinging the canoe into the wind. A roller crested over the left gunwale, sloshing over our legs and gear and destabilizing the canoe with a couple inches of shifting fluid.

As we paddled along the shoreline, accompanied by a handful of barking dogs from the village, I recalled what Sevareid had written about this juncture 76 years ago.

Five hundred miles beyond, across a vast stretch of wilderness, lay our goal, the North Atlantic Ocean. Could we do it?

We had to, for there could be no turning back, once we had left Norway House. We never could paddle back up any of the swift rivers that cascade to the bay, and hiking through the dense, impenetrable "bush country" couldn't be done. Suppose we smashed up our canoe in a rapid and lost our outfit, our food, our blankets and our matches and rifles— what then?

As Sevareid and Port looked back one last time at the beaches of Norway House, however, their perceptions were markedly different than ours: "Overalled and moccasined Cree braves, fat squaws and gurgling Indian babies, stared at us, and the white men and women cheered."

Despite the yearning to look back, and the instinctual desire to remain connected with this community that had been so welcoming, the lake required considerable vigilance. We were heavy and unstable, and the 500 miles we'd traveled on the Red River had not prepared us for rough open water. I was tense with foreboding, sensing that in an instant we could be overtaken by a wave coming out of nowhere, tossing us into the frigid water.

After several hours the wind subsided, and the sun broke through a thin layer of clouds. José and I set our paddles across our laps and breathed for what felt like the first time all afternoon.

We soon came upon a cable ferry that crossed our route, prohibiting further navigation up lake. At the portage landing a Cree couple and their three children sat together on exposed tree roots, eating cheese and crackers and drinking from a two-liter bottle of generic cola. They were all dressed up, as if for church or the theater.

They told us they were on their way to town for a day of shopping, but the ferry was temporarily shut down for repairs. And so they found it more comfortable to wait at the water's edge than at the side of the road. Apparently the weather, which felt cool and blustery to us, was scorching for the Cree.

Without asking if we wanted help, every member of the family, including the two-year-old boy, picked up a piece of our equipment—in his case a paddle three times his height—and began walking it down the trail.

LOST AND FOUND

Five miles beyond the ferry crossing, a thunderstorm burst from an angry cloud and honed in on us like a heat-seeking missile. We made for shore, hastily erected camp on a bed of mud between the water's edge and an impenetrable birch forest, and dove into the tent.

Mosquitoes had descended with the rain in ungodly swarms, and a dozen or so of them were in the tent, feasting on our clammy skin. This was our first uncomfortable encounter with mosquitoes. A late spring freeze had prevented them from spawning and given us one less hardship to endure on the Red River.

"Jesus, fuck, Jesus!" José slapped his body, thrashed, and shrieked, carrying on about the West Nile virus.

The mosquito-borne disease, known to cause flu-like symptoms lasting a few days, had recently arrived in Minnesota, where it was greeted by public health officials and the media with hand-wringing hysteria. I thought José was being ridiculous and told him so. Still, the kid was petrified.

I left the tent to prepare dinner while José manned the zipper. As with the mammoth flies, the mosquitoes seemed disinterested as I boiled water and added it to a pouch containing a dehydrated meal.

José watched through the screen as I savored a spoonful of what the packaging called Oriental Fried Rice. "Hey bro," he pleaded, "I'm starving in here. How about bringing José some of that grub? Help a brother out."

I was in no mood to help a brother out. A brother would have to leave the tent if he wanted to eat.

Around midnight, long after I had returned to the tent, José ventured out to cook for himself, wearing for the first time the protective clothing I had given him at the outset of the trip: a camo baseball cap with shoulder-length mosquito netting, a black zip-up windbreaker with a hood, and a headlamp.

As he waited the requisite five minutes for the lasagna to soak up liquid, José slapped mosquitoes, cussing loudly about the "diseased motherfuckers." Then he opened the pouch, jabbed his spoon into the steaming meal, and raised it to his lips beneath the mosquito netting. "Not bad," he offered, "not bad at all."

I could smell José's meal from inside the tent, and apparently the mosquitoes could too, as multitudes of them descended on our camp. José began to panic, shoveling food into his mouth and then begging me to let him return.

Back in the tent, José used his headlamp to hunt down the handful of insects that had followed him. Then, recalling his recently eaten meal-in-a-pouch, he lay back on his sleeping bag and proclaimed, "I ain't gonna lie, dawg, that was flame. That lasagna was damn good."

I awoke several times over the next few hours, certain every rustling leaf was a bear that had come to eat the scraps José had left strewn about the camp. When I emerged from the tent the following morning, it was obvious that I had been wrong to assume José was anything but responsible with his food waste. There wasn't a shred of garbage in sight, the stove and dishes were put away, and the food barrels were sealed tight.

I'd dreaded this part of the trip since first poring over the maps in Saint Paul. On this day we would seek the headwaters of the Echimamish, the 40-mile creek that connects Playgreen Lake and the Nelson River to the Hayes River. If we missed the headwaters, I worried we'd end up miles downstream, unable to fight our way back in the stout current. And Playgreen Lake, with its jagged shores, tight islands, and extended bays, made navigation exceptionally difficult.

Late in the day, as we struggled to stay abreast of waves that made the canoe shudder like a cold child, I remembered Sevareid's account of how he and Port had suffered vertigo while seeking the Echimamish. In fact, it was on Playgreen Lake that Sevareid experienced hypothermia for the first time. "Trying to watch the rollers," he wrote, "trying to follow the markers on the islands—we were rapidly becoming miserable. An aching pain crept into my cold legs to complete the anguish."

Our day was dry and sunny, but José and I were no less miserable. At one point we took advantage of a windbreak, resting to eat on the lee side of a small island. Parked in the calm pool, I reached into a food barrel for the trail mix and sunk my fingers into chilled goo. I looked down to find my right hand covered in the remains of José's lasagna. In his moment of panic, he had obviously jammed his garbage, cooking pot, and water purifier into the food barrel. A paste of rehydrated tomato sauce coated the inside of the barrel. The water purifier's parts were covered in sauce and scattered among the food packages.

"What the fuck!" I shouted. Then, as I tried to reconstruct the water purifier, I discovered that a vital piece of the mechanism was missing. I unleashed another string of expletives.

Back on the water after reaching a testy détente, I silently steered us to a small, round island covered by scrub pine trees. We quickly located a flat elevated slab that made for a natural campsite. And yet there was no sign of anyone having stayed there before: no fire ring nor ashes, no garbage nor woodpile, and certainly no footprints. All of which only added to my worry that we were off course.

José sensed my mood and grew even surlier. Later that night, he cleaned his dinner dishes by scraping the leftovers into the lake. I was nearly asleep when he entered the tent, pulled on his headphones, and played a CD at full volume. This would not have led to conflict had he not begun singing Avril Lavigne's "I'm with You," a sappy love song he knew I couldn't stand. I hoped a few minutes of quiet suffering would satisfy his lust for rebellion. Instead, he hit replay and continued his agonizingly off-key assault: "Won't you take me by the hand, take me somewhere new, I don't know who you are but I'm, I'm with you."

In a flash of rage I reached across his wiry body, trying to get my hands on the CD player. Soon we were rolling around the tent, struggling and pushing. "Shut up, please, shut the hell up," I pleaded. José just caterwauled in response, "I'm with you-oo."

It was as close as we would come to a brawl over the course of the journey. Unable to wrest the CD player from him, I ripped the headphones off his head. His dreadful performance ceased abruptly, and before long we were resting in an uneasy silence.

The following morning we emerged from the tent to find the campsite bathed in golden morning light, the surrounding forests and waters a sparkling wonderland. The bed of dry stone was much more comfortable than the mud we were used to, and I'd slept exceptionally well.

I walked the island's edge with a compass and a map, examining the water's flow for clues to our whereabouts. At the far side of the island I followed a floating tree trunk's progress as it bobbed downstream, losing sight of it beyond the curve of a channel. The Nelson traveled straight north here, but the Echimamish went east, the way of the trunk. Had I by dumb luck chosen a campsite near the headwaters of the Echimamish? The possibility that we weren't lost unburdened me. I yelled at José to wake up: "Bro, you're missing a beautiful morning! Let's get going! I think I know where we are!"

I sat down on an outcropping of the Canadian Shield a few feet above the crystal waters. I snapped photos, wrote in my journal, and penned a letter to a friend back home while waiting for José to complete his customary morning process. Then, just when I was beginning to relax, I spied the refuse from José's dinner, a field of macaroni noodles clinging to a moss-covered rock in three inches of water beneath my dangling feet. The anger returned.

When José didn't emerge from the tent in 10 minutes, I began taking it down. He crawled out of the deflated shelter looking drowsy and bewildered. I confronted him about the food in the water. "It could have attracted bears, and now everyone who comes after us will have to deal with your garbage."

I went on and on, and when I finally concluded this tirade, José asked me if I was finished. Then he went off. He called me a "hippie environmentalist douchebag," and told me to "loosen the fuck up." "We're out here in the middle of nowhere, bro," he continued. "You wanted this, you asked me to come here. There ain't no turning back now, might as well have some goddamn fun."

I heard him out while packing up camp. We loaded the canoe and held tight to shore. I felt sure the water would take us east once we let go of the downed pine to which we clung.

Just then a pair of Cree fishermen drifted past in a motorboat. They were dressed in identical rain jackets and peered at us solemnly from beneath black hoods.

"Echimamish?" I called.

The guy steering the outboard lifted his chin to the east.

"Let's go," said José, impatient with my uncertainty. "The Cree brother said it was that way."

We pushed off and braided along with the current through dozens of uncharted islands. After a few miles we still hadn't found the channel. I began to wonder if the men in the motorboat had pointed us in the wrong direction. Increasingly frustrated and disoriented from all the twists and switchbacks, we finally came upon a sign nailed to a tree that read "York Boat Route." While it seemed to point in the right direction, the arrow below these words directed us against the current. We held up in a tangle of downed pines to consult the map and compass again. Nothing made sense. North was where I thought South should be, and East and West kept switching sides.

Just when I was beginning to lose my mind, José reminded me of something the Boss had said back in the harbormaster's courtyard. "When you get near the Echimamish there are a thousand different ways to go. They all lead to the same place. Continue to the east and you can't miss it."

We struggled against a swift flow for half a mile or so. Then, inexplicably and without changing course, we were washed down an easy rapids and deposited in a narrow creek surrounded to the horizon by bronze cattails, willows, and lush beds of wild rice.

For the next two days we paddled this unassuming artery, stopping often to haul the canoe over beaver dams that towered more than two body lengths over the water. At some point during the second day we noticed the boat migrating backward when our paddles were at rest. I had never seen a river's flow change direction before, but there was no other explanation.

Later that night, in the light of the midnight sun, I thumbed through my copy of *Canoeing with the Cree*, recalling that Sevareid had noted this strange phenomenon as well. In fact, the shifting flow of the Echimamish had contributed to Sevareid and Port going astray.

We were lost—no doubt about it. We sat and stared at each other as the sweat ran into our eyes. On our maps there showed no indication of the reedy lake which circled away before us. The Echimamish had meandered into this body of water and despite two careful rounds of the shore line, we could find no outlet. The beautifully fringed lake smiled on in the September sunshine, while our despair grew.

With freeze-up only weeks away, the boys could not afford to waste time. Sevareid struggled to maintain his composure. And then finally, after methodically retracing their steps for 15 miles of "painful traveling, combining paddling with wading in soft mud and dragging the canoe," they found their way back to the Echimamish.

The fact that it was now late June meant that we were not similarly pressed for time, not in peril of being stranded by the freeze nor lost in the wilderness. And yet the Echimamish inspired dread in José as well. I saw panic on his face each time we approached another beaver dam. He would gingerly step onto the logs, so as not to disturb the beavers who were going to "fuck me up for climbing all over their crib." In the calm pools between dams the beavers swam close to our bow, banged their wide, smooth tails against the surface, and dove beneath the canoe. José flinched at the crack of those tails. "Oh hell no," he moaned, "them bitches is trying to fuck a nigga up."

As we dragged the canoe up and over these logjams, José increasingly understood the seriousness of the commitment he had made, and the incontrovertible fact that there was no turning back. This realization aside, José's shoulders were throbbing so painfully he wasn't sure he could continue. I remembered the pills we'd purchased in Winnipeg. I pulled the first aid kit from a Duluth pack and found the medicine inside.

"Here you go, bro," I said, pushing two tablets through the foil backing and handing them up to José.

José swallowed the pills and returned to his intermittent paddling. The lack of power coming from the front of the canoe combined with the formidable resistance provided by thick grasses made our going extremely slow. With no clear channel through the foliage, we bushwhacked. Every few minutes I stood in the stern to verify we were on course to reconnect with the Echimamish.

Twenty minutes after downing the pills, José was hardly moving his paddle through the water. I implored him to dig deep, but before long he was slumped over to the side, out like a light. Frustrating as it was to power the canoe alone through those relentless grasses, I was relieved by the silence. My resentment of José had been building since we crossed the border, but now I could feel it softening.

We camped early that evening, alongside a sedentary pool between two beaver lodges. With the medicine still circulating in his blood, José slept soundly, unbothered by the incessant banging of beaver tails.

After another day of difficult paddling, we arrived the following afternoon at Painted Stone Portage, a 30-foot ridge of the Canadian Shield separating the Nelson and Hayes River watersheds. Under gathering storm clouds, José and I went about our duties silently, hauling our loads across a pathway that paralleled a sort of log railroad for York boats.

Our experience on the Hayes began peacefully the next morning. We paddled still green waters 10 canoe lengths wide flanked by dramatic rock outcroppings. José watched the whirlpools pirouetting beside the canoe with each languid stroke. "This ain't shit," he proclaimed, entirely unaware of the challenges ahead. "This is actually pretty dope."

When the sun was three fingers above the tree line, the

Hayes opened into Robinson Lake, five bays connected end to end like a string of pearls shining in the metallic afternoon.

At the mouth of the second bay we struggled against a bruising headwind that drove whitecaps over the bow. I knew we couldn't stay on the water, but I was also afraid to turn back, worried that any deviation from our present course would cause the canoe to swamp. I'd seen a single campsite on the lake, an elevated peninsula a half mile behind us, and I decided to go for it. I told José to get low and back-paddle hard. We rocked left and took a drenching over the gunwales, but somehow we managed to swing the bow due west, into the wind.

Surfing atop the surge, we quickly made it to the peninsula and crashed onto a boulder field at the base of a craggy slab. José scampered up the wall and dragged the packs into the clearing as I lifted them overhead. Then we hauled the canoe up and flipped it onto some prickly brush. I screamed at José through the tornadic growl. "Put up the tent, bro. I'll collect some wood."

I dropped down to the boulder field to gather driftwood that had washed up on the lakeshore. These weathered old logs would burn hot for hours. Then, as quickly as it had come up, the gale died.

I climbed up to the clearing and put down the driftwood. José stood with the unfurled tent hanging under his arm, transfixed by something at his feet.

I hurried over to him. "What up, bro? You alright?"

He kneeled and picked up an eagle feather, twisting the

black plume between his thumb and forefinger. He examined it closely and then exclaimed, "Finally."

José later told me he had cleared the area for the tent and was about to throw it down when he noticed the feather at his toes. He swore it materialized out of thin air. We pondered the role of the wind in guiding us to that campsite, how it had stymied us with sudden ferocity and then ceased as soon as the feather appeared.

José wiped his cheeks with the back of his hands and examined them to confirm that he had shed real tears. Then, for the first time since his father's overdose, he broke down and sobbed.

HELL'S GATE

Paddling glassy Robinson Lake the following morning, José reflected on his eagle feather. His initial elation gave way to saltiness about what he thought of as an excessive wait for a spiritual gift he'd long deserved. "I know tons of motherfuckers who got their feathers at, like, 13 years old," he raged, "and they're assholes who don't give a shit about nothing. I didn't get mine till I was 20. Even you got your feather first."

I tried to reassure him, explaining that his feather had actually come way before mine. "Do the math. I might have received that feather first on this trip, but I'm 18 years older than you, so it actually took longer for my feather to come."

"I wasn't going to say anything, bro, but that really hurt," he replied. "Even the white guy got an eagle feather before me. The white guy!"

Robinson Lake is the bottom rung of a four-step ladder of relatively small bodies of water that tilts northeast to Oxford Lake, a 35-mile-long, island-freckled giant that hung above our current position on the map like an anvil.

To achieve the next rung, Logan Lake, we would have to portage nearly a mile around Robinson Falls.

In addition to its intimidating length, the Robinson portage offered no obvious trailhead opening into the woods, and the landing was a steamy muskeg bog thick with black flies and mosquitoes.

If we hoped to make the portage in just one trip we would have to lighten our load. With mosquitoes feasting on my limbs, I made a desperate decision to reduce the burden by burning our garbage. I set the trash bag on a rise of hardened mud and held a lighter to it. The plastic melted open and the collection of wet foil sacks flared, but ultimately the trash refused to burn. We would have to make the trip twice. I waved a few wisps of smoke toward my chest, hoping the noxious scent would repel the swarm. Then I left the garbage on the ground and helped José slip into two Duluth packs—one on his chest and one on his back. Finally, I flipped the canoe onto my shoulders and walked along the remnant of a handcar railway that once transported York boats over the falls, found the trailhead, and plunged headlong into the brush.

As I walked along the neglected trail, overgrown with thistles that drew red lines across my legs, I was dying to throw the canoe off my shoulders and scrape the black biting sleeves from my arms. Instead, I let the insects do their worst and placed one boot in front of the other as fast as my dissociating mind would push them.

I watched my mottled shadow against the green foliage

at my feet for distraction while a mosquito buzzed into my left ear and lowered its proboscis into my eardrum. It took a good long sip while I screamed, grinding my ear against my shoulder until the buzzing ceased and a drop of blood slithered out.

I scrambled over rough trunks of fallen trees, balancing the canoe on my shoulders, carefully guiding my unwieldy load through the tangle of vegetation. Mosquitoes landed on my cheeks and looked me in the eye, drawing blood with impunity. I listened to the rush of Robinson Falls without curiosity or hint of pleasure, focused intently on putting one foot in front of the other.

Finally, the trees opened to blue sky and I heaved the canoe into the calm pool of Logan Lake. I collapsed against the yoke, straining to replenish my blood with oxygen.

Headed back up the trail not five minutes later, I could hear José long before I saw him. "Fuck you bitches! Fuck you little niggas. I'm going to fuck you up!"

I ran back up the trail until I reached him, not halfway across the portage. His arms were asleep from the pinch of the pack straps, rendering him helpless against the blood-sucking swarm. His face was anemic and perspiring, his neck and shoulders covered in pink welts.

I grabbed the pack off his front and we raced against madness to Logan Lake. We dropped the packs, then trudged back to the top of the portage, where two more awaited. We collected the half-burnt sack of trash, along with the remaining packs, paddles, and life jackets, and once again ran the agonizing gauntlet.

I reached Logan Lake first and waited by the canoe, watching as José locomoted down the trail, tripped backward along with his hefty Duluth pack into the waiting boat, clambered into the bow, and thrashed his paddle against the swampy pool, screaming psychotically: "Let's get the fuck out of here, bro. I lost my goddamn glasses, but I don't give a shit. Let's go, let's GO. Paddle harder, nigga. No fucking way I'm going back in there!"

The little carnivores followed as we pushed through the haze hovering over Logan Lake—the result, we would learn later, of forest fires. While I dreaded returning to the scene of the carnage we'd just endured, I tried to persuade José that we should go back for his glasses. After all, we would soon be entering a stretch of the trip where we would encounter whitewater every day.

"Them little bitches raped me," he cried in a falsetto that suggested real trauma. "No way I'm going back there. Fuck that."

Later that day, when our memory of the death march had begun to recede, José and I talked about how we both had felt watched along the portage—not by a supernatural presence, but rather by a man who seemed to be lurking behind the brush and trees. At the end of the portage we had even found evidence of a crude campsite: a fire ring filled with ash and a plastic tarp tied between two trees, sheltering a couple of moldy blankets, fishing nets, and an old pair of hiking boots. How anyone could survive even one night in that place was beyond our comprehension, but it certainly seemed as if someone was doing just that.

When evening arrived we found a campsite and, after a dinner of trail mix and lemon Kool-Aid, sought refuge within the protective cocoon of the tent. Neither of us slept much, however, twitching all night in response to the sharp chomping of no-see-ums. The tiny insects slipped through the mosquito netting and treated our weary skin like prime rib at a buffet.

I sat up half the night, slapping my neck, writing in my journal, and reading *Canoeing with the Cree*. Sevareid didn't mention the Robinson portage in his narrative, perhaps because he and Port were lost again as they passed through the area. After poking around Robinson Lake, the boys were unable to find their portage, and with each passing hour their situation grew increasingly dire. There are no place names in this section of Sevareid's narrative, likely an indication that the boys were lost, and increasingly aware of the dreadful consequences that would ensue when the waterways froze.

To make matters worse for the bewildered pair, Manitoba was enduring a terrible drought in the late summer of 1930, and "fire, the scourge of the pine country, had swept through an immense area" only a few days before they arrived on the scene. They floated past "row on row of black trees grim in their deathlike silence."

Perhaps it was the macabre landscape of the Hayes headwaters that convinced them to heed the advice of a trapper they'd met back in Norway House. They'd instinctively trusted Karl Sherman, "a young, ruddy-faced Norwegian trapper who, in his twelve years there, had learned to know nearly every stream of any consequence in the region." Sherman had reported that the Hayes was exceptionally shallow that year, and advised them to find an alternative route.

Sevareid and Port eventually concluded that their very survival depended on traveling eastward, across a 50-mile maze of lakes and portages, to Gods River, an artery that paralleled and eventually joined the Hayes. Sherman had told the boys that there was plenty of flow in Gods River. But soon after setting out from the Hayes, they were desperately disoriented.

Sevareid and Port were eventually rescued by three men paddling through Robinson Lake. "Manned by two Indians and carrying a white man who sat reading in the center," the canoe stopped at the boys' campsite. As luck would have it, the three were en route to Gods Lake, the source of the Gods River, and they invited the boys to follow. Over the next several days, Sevareid and Port struggled to keep pace with the Cree paddlers, slogging through a handful of portages that surely could be compared to what we had endured.

> [Those portages] almost broke our backs. . . . In the first place, our canoe could not be carried by one of us. The middle thwart was missing, we had no portage yoke and our paddles were not long enough to serve as shoulder braces. Each portage meant two

trips apiece for us. First we would load each other up with about one hundred and fifty pounds of outfit and stagger the distance. Gasping, we hurried back and threw the canoe to our shoulders.

Traveling those four days across Cree homelands, Sevareid gained an appreciation for the Indians' grace and strength. In fact, this section of *Canoeing with the Cree* is arguably the first time he represents Native people respectfully.

It was a gorgeous experience, living with the Crees. . . . There seemed to be something about each portage that put frenzy in the hearts of the Indians. Within two minutes after beaching they would have about two hundred and fifty pounds apiece on their backs, and away they trotted as though their very lives depended upon speed.

Marveling at the stark contrast that arrived with sunrise the following morning, we dipped our paddles into the glassy channel where the Hayes exited Logan Lake and flowed to the northwest. The bugs had vanished and the still air, cool and refreshing, was a healing salve.

In the serene morning light I watched José as he reached and pulled the water. His physique, which only weeks before had resembled cooked linguine, had grown muscular, rounded, and sinewy. His neck had thickened and his torso broadened.

As I observed him, I wondered if the difficulties faced by Native youth across the continent—drug abuse and suicide, diabetes and obesity, the whole long legacy of genocide—could be addressed, at least in part, by helping young people travel across their ancestral lands under their own power.

José wasn't out of the woods yet, to be sure. When he returned to Saint Paul he would face significant challenges. But as we glided on the marble reflection of cotton clouds, drifting along on a sanguine current, we devised grand plans for a program that would reintroduce Native youth to their history, language, culture, and spirituality, all by way of canoeing.

Around midday I emerged from a daydream, famished, and wondered how long it had been since José, slumped over in the bow, had placed his paddle in the water.

"I'm so hungry. I'm gonna go catch a deer," he groaned. "And when I catch that deer I'm funna ride it to White Castle."

We agreed that I would continue to paddle while he fired up the stove and cooked ramen noodles in the bow. I made real progress in the stillness of the afternoon, ripping into the mirrored surface with a strength that flowed effortlessly from my core. I loved the changes weeks of hardcore physical exertion had made to my body. My arms were cut and lean, and my stomach, once obscured by a supple layer of flesh, was now flat and defined. I wondered how I could ever be happy living a more sedentary life.

The salty aroma of beef-flavored ramen drifted back to me. José poured the cooked noodles into two cups and hesitated before handing one back to me. "You know what would be flame, bro?" he asked. "Jailhouse food."

José explained that he'd learned to cook jailhouse food from his brother D. In some of the correctional facilities in which D had spent his childhood, the cells contained small stoves for warming drinks. The inmates weren't supposed to use them for cooking, José continued, but they were resourceful. "You take your ramen noodles, boil them up, and then fry the noodles in a little grease. Just add a little onion or a spoonful of sofrito. I ain't gonna lie, bro, jailhouse food is flame."

He set his hot cup on one of the food barrels and popped open the latch on the other. He dug around for the small unopened bottle of vegetable oil buried at the bottom. Soon the air was alive with the fragrance of sizzling fat and starch. By the time he refilled our cups with his version of jailhouse food, I had paddled alone for an hour, covering some three river miles.

It didn't take long for me to comprehend José's lust for this kind of meal. Intoxicating and delicious, the fried-in-fat strands of simple carbohydrates were a tasty shot of dietary heroin. After the meal, I rested on the V of the rear gunwales, high on gluten and MSG, watching puffy clouds form and dissipate in the sky.

We'd been drifting for some time when a roar akin to a freight train bearing down on us alerted me to a nightmare. We'd passed unwittingly into Hell's Gate, a narrow canyon through which the collective drainage of billions of acres is squeezed on its journey to the sea. And we were just seconds from the maelstrom.

I stuck my paddle deep into the speeding turmoil, causing the canoe's nose to ram between two boulders. Had this split-second maneuver not succeeded, we almost surely would have been pummeled to death in the roaring chute.

If there was a portage around Hell's Gate, we were already past it. The trailhead would have been on the low-lying banks of an island that cut the river in two as it accelerated through the canyon. To attempt the crossing from the boulders where we pondered our fate would have been a painful form of suicide, and walls of stone rising up from the water meant there were no bottoms we might walk. Our only chance would be to climb the sheer granite face towering above us and puppeteer the canoe through the raging canyon below with 50-foot lengths of rope.

José leaped onto a narrow ledge inches above the waterline and ascended the spindly rock, clinching the stern rope in his teeth. After a few deft grabs and pulls, he stood on the ridgeline.

I struggled up the sheer embankment to join him, the bow rope secured around my waist. I made the summit by jamming my boots and hands into a two-inch fissure that drew a steep slant up the rock like the chart of a rising stock. I hauled myself over the crest and stood on quivering legs.

I scouted Hell's Gate from the lofty vantage. The ivory chute barreled straight down the canyon for about a hundred yards, at which point the channel widened and the waters swirled in a mélange of silver-tipped waves and foaming black eddies.

We yanked the ropes upstream to dislodge the canoe, then guided it around the rocks that had held it in place. As the canoe entered the fierce flow it skipped lightly upon the surface, floating like antimatter on a cushion of velocity.

We began to guide the boat along slowly on the rushing waters, navigating the knotty pines on the cliff by passing the ropes from hand to hand. I took cautious half steps, anxiously considering every move. It was clear that a single misstep could amount to the total loss of our gear, and the ruination of the canoe. We were at least three days from the Oxford House First Nations Reserve, the nearest human settlement. By water, that is. By land, bushwhacking through the impassable forest, it would easily take 10 days.

Halfway through the canyon, our task was made more difficult by a jagged shoreline that deflected unpredictable currents into the side of the canoe. Every few steps we were treated to a terrifying preview of what would happen if we allowed these accelerated flows to have their way: the stern drifted toward the middle, causing tremendous hydrologic pressure to build against the side of the canoe, threatening to flood the gunwales, tear the ropes from our hands, and send the partially submerged craft careening sideways down the rapids.

"Hold the stern!" I shouted repeatedly. "Pull it in! We have to keep the canoe in line with the current!" José walked behind me, silently absorbing my imperious commands.

He had tied the rope around his wrist, forcing him to skirt the edge of the cliff to avoid getting wrapped up in the trees. This precarious maneuvering—ducking and swinging from overhanging branches—caused him to take his eye off the canoe, allowing slack and tricky currents to wreak havoc.

Suddenly the stern angled sideways to the rushing water, yanking José to the edge of the cliff with shocking force. He strained against the rope, falling onto his backside in an attempt to arrest the killer momentum. The canoe tilted at an angle to the onrush. A wave piled against the sidewall and climbed over the gunwale, drenching our gear.

José backpedaled on a slippery bed of leaves and lichens, but could not arrest his skid. Another few seconds and he would be pulled over the cliff. In a moment of adrenaline-fueled epiphany, I saw what had to be done: "Let go of the rope!" I shouted.

Confusion joined panic on José's face, but he responded immediately to the counterintuitive suggestion. Straining against the rope with his left hand to create slack, he wriggled and shook his right. The rope sprung free and traveled like fly line across the canoe, alighting on the roaring river. With amazing grace, the free end of the canoe came around, caught the tender twist of the eddy, and taxied to safety in a quiet alcove near the shore.

José watched the last stage of this drama unfold with a horrified expression. He would later reflect that until I'd yelled, it hadn't occurred to him to release the rope to save his life. "Ain't funna lie, bro. I thought I was a goner."

We slid on our soles down a gentle slope to the water, then shoved the canoe into the eddy, where it rotated so the bow was downstream.

We pushed through the eddy's grip. I leaned on my paddle, fighting currents that pushed and pulled, until we settled several miles downstream in the calm pools of Opiminegoka Lake.

A mile or two south of Wapanipanis Falls, the Hayes split into two channels surrounding a nameless wetland with towering grasses. I lingered at the fork, consulting a map, our compass, and the GPS. But neither of these waterways seemed to lead to the falls. I searched for clues: a quick ripple of current, the distant hush of falling water, an intuitive pull toward one opening or the other. I scanned the horizon for the blue snake of a flowing stream. A cold sweat gathered on my forehead.

José was no help. One day after surviving Hell's Gate, he was silent and in a foul mood. He dipped his paddle ineffectually, his headphones loud and tight.

I soon found my directional beacon in a bald eagle soaring toward the westward channel. I relaxed at the sight, enthralled by the raptor's otherworldly majesty. Recalling the famous story of Leonard Peltier—the American Indian Movement member who, following eagles through the hills of the Pine Ridge Reservation, escaped the largest manhunt in FBI history—I took the eagle as a divine message to paddle west.

Over the following hours, I came to see José's dramatic reactions to stressful situations as symptoms of intergenerational trauma, which is often cited as the fundamental reason Native Americans continue to suffer from many health issues, such as high rates of suicide and drug and alcohol addiction.

I thought back to a lecture I'd attended some two months before José and I set out. It was delivered by Darlene Kawennanoron Johnson, a Mohawk therapist and researcher, at a Native American mental health convention. She described how pain and trauma were passed down from generation to generation, resulting in low self-esteem and cultural shame. She made a particularly compelling case for the notion that the loss of language, traditions, and culture resulted in a loss of spirit, which manifested itself in a lack of extended family and community bonding, increased domestic violence, child and elder abuse, and internalized oppression.

As I thought back on how this matched my experiences in Native American communities across the country, it occurred to me that I had my own experience with intergenerational trauma. As a child, my mother had been hidden in a Catholic boarding school in the mountains of southern France as Nazis took over her country. She survived several attempts by German operatives to discover and deport Jews at the school.

Before she was placed in this boarding school, when she was 5 years old, her father, 35 years old at the time, was captured by the Gestapo and tortured to death in a public square. After the war, my grandmother left for America and my mother was placed in a series of homes. It was only years later that they were reunited in New York.

I had conducted extensive interviews with my grandmother before she died in 2005, at age 93. Her name was Paulette Oppert, but her grandchildren all knew her as *Maman*. I recalled the pain in *Maman*'s eyes as she spoke in her thick French accent into my tape recorder, telling the story of the day in 1943 that she said marked the beginning of the end of my mother's childhood, the day she found out her father had been killed by the Nazis.

As a young boy, I never understood the root of my mother's rage, nor why I often suffered crippling anxiety in her presence. I didn't understand why I had only a handful of relatives at family gatherings, nor why I was warned by my mother, from the time I could talk, never to tell anyone I was Jewish. I never understood why she didn't teach me to speak French, nor why she hoarded staples and dry goods. And then as I grew up, I came to recognize that nearly all my closest friends descended from survivors of genocide: Jews, Native Americans, and Armenians among them.

Increasingly agitated, I watched my paddle disturb the silty murk that hung suspended above the bottom. I wished José would talk to me, or at least paddle with enough effort to hasten our meanderings. I was tired of thinking about how my mother's grief had attached itself to my bones.

Trapped in the isolation brought on by José's silence, my mind moved on to happier childhood memories, of my mother reading me bedtime stories. There were two books I thought back to now, each of them favorites from her own upbringing: *Pancakes Paris*, a story about the liberation of the French capital by American soldiers (who fed starving children by distributing pancake mix and maple syrup), and *The Little Prince*, Antoine de Saint-Exupéry's famous novella, which was published the year my grandfather was murdered.

I read *The Little Prince* several times as a child, and with each reading my understanding of the book grew. But the impact of those earliest readings was never equaled. Even as a five-year-old I felt the little prince's deep and painful attachment to the red rose, the one thing of beauty that grew on his asteroid. He cared for her day and night, lovingly providing water and warmth, and yet she didn't return his affection. Without her, the little prince was all alone in the universe.

I remembered reading somewhere that Saint-Exupéry had based the drawings of the little prince included in the book on images of himself as a child. Much of the story is said to have been based on hallucinations the aviator experienced in the winter of 1935, after he crashed his plane in the Sahara. He wandered for four days without water, before being saved by a Bedouin who administered a native rehydration treatment.

One of the mirages Saint-Exupéry saw while struggling through the dunes was that of a talking fox. This fox delivers a key line in the novella, and I found myself pondering it as I paddled: "One sees clearly only with the heart," says the fox. "Anything essential is invisible to the eyes."

While José and I were raised in very different circumstances, I was beginning to understand one of the factors that had brought us together. When he was just seven years old, county social workers took José from his mother and placed him in the first of a series of foster homes. From that time forward he fended for himself, shuffling from family members to the homes of strangers and then on to group homes and juvenile detention centers.

Like a child soldier, José fought often and ran constantly. On this canoe trip, he was once again fending for himself. I could see when he wanted to run, and when he wanted to fight. But I was the only one there to fight, and the simple truth was that he needed me. And then it was also true that there was nowhere to run.

I didn't tell José we had lost our way until the silver mists of Wapanipanis Falls rose above the reeds. At the time I was disappointed, as I had followed the eagle the long way around the wetland. Looking back, the long way was almost surely the best way, as the kind of reflection it permitted would ultimately lead to the success of our journey.

I trudged around Wapanipanis's 20-foot drop with the canoe on my shoulders, my boots filling with soft white sand. On my return trip up the trail I saw that the fine ivory substance cut a 20-yard-wide swath through the forest. This was the winter road depicted as a faint grey line on the map, a track running some 150 miles between Norway

House and Oxford House, the Cree settlement we hoped to reach within the next two or three days.

José and I explored the surreal landscape, finding along the route a boneyard of industrial truck parts: shredded tires, mufflers, rusting axles, windshield wipers, oil filters, and catalytic converters. In the soupy haze generated by distant forest fires, shards of shattered windshield sparkled like rubies in the penetrating sunlight.

The length of a football field beyond the falls, a short yellow school bus sat on blocks at the edge of the sand. Upon inspection we found the interior modified with a woodstove and chimney, along with a sink, a cutting board, and a cot. The seats and the engine well had been gutted and trash strewn about the floor. I studied the scene, home now to a lethargic colony of black flies, and couldn't help but think of Chris McCandless, the kid who'd starved to death in a similar bus in Alaska, his story forming the basis for *Into the Wild*.

My reverie was broken by the cadence of José's voice, his words sounding like a poetic summation of his recent past.

I am a U.S. fugitive, shot a man but did not kill him. Self-defense, bitch did me wrong. Will not do jail time, rather die, running twenty-nine days and two years now. Hitched ice road to bus. Arrived 3-3-06. Fear law closing in. Leaving 7-20-06, seeking new camp. Short food, supplies. Unsure what next. If you find this, remember I was here.

I was momentarily confused, then realized that José was reading a paragraph scrawled in black Sharpie on the wall of the bus, between a cot and a window frame. I wondered if this could possibly be the man we thought we had sensed at Robinson portage.

We spent the next hour or so paddling over undemanding rapids, until we arrived in a back bay of Oxford Lake, the 30-mile expanse that stood between us and Oxford House. I was eager to reach the settlement, as I hoped the expanded social contact would relieve some of the animosity that had been building in José since we'd parted ways with the Boss and his family five days earlier.

The ease of travel on the last stretch of the Hayes had relaxed me considerably, but this state vanished when we were greeted by a sinister-looking front hanging over the mouth of the channel. It blotted out the sun and unleashed a furious headwind, arresting our progress in a pool surrounded by boulders.

When the day began I had planned to paddle halfway up the monster lake before making camp. It was late afternoon already, but at that latitude, where dusk lingered past midnight, there was plenty of daylight left.

We paddled for an hour or so more, to where the bay widened out significantly. When cool raindrops began to fall, we pulled to a nearby point. I pitched the tent in a small clearing surrounded by pines, and we decided to call it a night.

OXFORD LAKE

I awoke shivering in the opaque golden glow of the tent, my breath curling above my face. The temperature had plummeted overnight as a strong cold front moved through. I could hear a powerful northerly blow out on the bay, but our spot on the rock was well sheltered by the surrounding pines.

José abbreviated his morning ritual when I told him the tailwind meant we had a chance to make Oxford House before nightfall. Given the challenges associated with paddling on such an immense body of water, my assertion was arguably bluster. But I was eager to make contact with the Cree community, and powerfully tired of José's company.

We loaded the canoe and pulled the spray deck taut, fastening it to the black Velcro patches beneath the gunwales. We suited up in layers, rain gear, and stocking caps, then slid onto our seats, fixing the skirting under our armpits and sheltering our bodies beneath the cobalt tarp.

As we paddled along the north shore of a large island and out into the open water, I took comfort in the meager survival kits José and I carried in the breast pockets of our life jackets. The chaotic waters and blooming skies soon obliterated any sense of horizon. I navigated a chain of dense green islands on a northeasterly heading, then stared into the abyss of a five-mile, wind-ravaged crossing. With José incommunicado beneath his headphones, I had only the tempest for company.

Struggling to repel a panic attack as vast thunderheads gathered along the north shore of the lake, I joined José in electronic oblivion for the first time all summer, pulling my iPod from its waterproof pouch and pushing the earbuds in. I pumped the volume up until music dominated the screeching breath of Mother Nature.

I soon realized that what I had taken to be the north shore of Oxford Lake was not a shore at all, but rather the coast of a clear-cut island several miles long. Grey mists hung above the lifeless flat, lending the thousands of stumps upon it an eerie spectral glow.

I counted 12 separate thunderheads in a straight squall, blooming like colossal roses over the forest to the near northeast. If these conditions endured, the almighty hand at our backs would push us to Oxford House by evening. But then one after another, the thunderheads burst, spewing downdrafts that whipped whitecaps over the canoe, forcing us to seek the pebbled sanctuary of a lone islet.

As José extricated himself from the spray deck and stumbled to shore on unsteady knees, he fiddled with his headphone jack, sullen as a newborn with an empty bottle.

We hauled the canoe high up on the beach to keep the waves from washing it out to sea.

Drenched from the waist down, our bare legs exposed to the stinging wind, a fearful discomfort descended on the beach. José blew into his hands and clutched his chest. I felt sorry for him; after several weeks out, he still didn't know how to build a fire.

I quickly identified an abundance of ready relief in the weathered driftwood tangled against the tree line. We gathered a thigh-high pile and, with a touch of my lighter to a crisp ring of birch bark, ignited a blaze. A ferocious heat soon curled the hair on our calves.

It would have been easy to call it a day and stay here for the night, but I was determined to test our limits. I unfurled the map on the beach, setting stones on the corners to keep it in place. If we were willing to add two or three miles to the route, I saw that we could avoid open water by weaving through a chain of islands. While this alternative route would likely deliver us to the village without incident, it would mean doing without the strong breeze, which had once again shifted to our backs.

On a straight-line course, the little island we had landed on was the last safe harbor on the way to Oxford House. We would be completely exposed along the way, and often at least a mile from the nearest land. Swamping out there would result in the sinking of the canoe, and the loss of all but the bare-bones emergency survival kits tucked into our life jackets, which contained just a signal mirror, a compass, duct tape, fire starter, fishing line, and a lens magnifier. Still, I was undeterred.

After an hour's break, we sealed our radiating bodies under the spray deck, paddled hard around a point, and swung into the curling surf. The advancing clouds stalled to our north, blowing up a surge of water that lifted the canoe eight feet above a trough, and then pushed us down into it with the thrust of an outboard. At the tops of these swells I could barely make out the metallic sheen of the distant village. The sight of Oxford House cemented my resolve, even as our hands cramped around our paddles.

José would later tell me how furious he was about the dangerous choices I'd made that day. But for the next five miles, riding the tops of those rollers, I was euphoric, immersed completely in the rush.

Then all hell broke loose, and we found ourselves trapped in the narrow gap between two thunderstorms. A bracing headwind replaced the tailwind, forcing whitecaps over the bow and onto the spray deck. Freezing rain pelted our cheeks. In constantly shifting currents, we confronted threats from every direction: swells breaching our gunwales from the left and right, and fast-moving rollers overtaking us from behind, sucking the canoe beneath the sizzling surface as they washed past.

After an hour of pure adrenaline-fueled panic, José and I gasped for breath and leaned hard on our paddles, scraping grooves into the sides of the canoe. My eyes sought land, even as I knew well that the nearest island was more than a mile to the south. I prayed for our lives, imagining my kids back in Saint Paul receiving the news that their father was missing, presumed dead.

We finally breached the ivory points of Oxford Lake's eastern bay at dusk. The brigade of thunderstorms had marched past, leaving in its wake clear skies and a gentle tailwind. The village was still seven miles away, and our tanks were empty. But we continued lowering our paddles into the lingering chop.

Eventually the squat, corrugated community of Oxford House dialed into focus. A mile or so from landfall we spotted a red dot on the horizon, quickly closing the distance between us. Soon we realized that this was a small motorboat, headed at us on a collision course.

Fifty yards from impact, the little fishing boat veered away, skipping off atop the waves. Its lone occupant wore a sparkling cherry-red motorcycle helmet. José and I laughed, wondering if the helmet was perhaps the outdated headgear of a tribal coast guard uniform. Our question would be answered the following afternoon, when we saw this eccentric local wearing the same helmet as he marched around town: walking out of the grocery store carrying a bucket of chicken, and under the baking sun alongside the village's dusty main road.

Not until we could make out the cracks on the walls of the Northern Store, the large warehouse outlet at the center of the village, did we finally relax, knowing we had made it safely to Oxford House. The sun fell behind the waterline behind us, casting the settlement in brilliant amber. Before pulling to shore we lingered on the glassy liquid, considering where we might camp. There is a protocol to follow when entering a remote Native community. Outsiders are kept under the watchful eyes of the wary residents as law enforcement is bare bones or nonexistent. I wondered who would be around at that late hour.

Thinking it might contain a solution, I dug out a book I'd carried along the entire trip, a guidebook of sorts called *Wilderness Rivers of Manitoba: Journey by Canoe through the Land Where the Spirit Lives*, the pages of which had been glued together since we'd capsized in the Red River on the very first day. Somewhere south of Winnipeg, a single page of this book had baked open—the page on which authors Hap Wilson and Stephanie Aykroyd describe their night at Oxford House. I located the passage and read it aloud:

> On reaching the reserve settlement we were told that it might be to our advantage to camp along the beach across the lake from the village. Good advice. It was a little unsettling to learn that the Indian kids sometimes pilfer tent sites and lob rocks at white visitors.

"That's some racist shit, bro," José growled in response. "You assuming these Indians is gonna throw rocks and steal from you cuz you're white." I detected in his voice a desire to paddle into the Native community alone, in order to avoid being associated with a racist white guy.

I explained quietly that I was reading from a book, not expressing my opinion. Then I showed him the cover and he seized on the name of its author, whom he would refer to as "old boy racist Hap" for the remainder of the trip.

Oxford House sat on a grassy, litter-strewn hill above the narrow bay. On the opposite side of the bay, a flat sandy beach reflected like a jewel in the day's last light. This beach would have made an ideal campsite, but after a number of days together, we wanted more company. We decided to make camp on a small plateau halfway up the village hill.

As I kicked aside popsicle wrappers and a flattened two-liter plastic bottle to clear a spot for the tent, we heard the growl and bang of an old car rumbling over the crest above us. I watched as José walked up the hill to the running Impala and engaged a young Cree couple. Then José shook the driver's hand, walked around the car, opened the rusted rear passenger door, and got in. The Impala drove off, a cloud of dust lingering over the spot where José had stood a moment ago.

While he was away I finalized our camp, securing the rain fly and fastening the metal collars on the food barrels, which I secured in light of the growing number of feral dogs at the shore below. I peeled off my boots and socks, revealing shriveled pale skin. I rested in the tent, writing in my journal and watching the endless last light, until the sunlight faded out around 2:00 a.m.

Long after I had begun wondering if I would ever see

José again, the rumble returned up on the hill, and I heard him call for me to "come meet the people," the thrill in his voice reminiscent of the hyperactive 15-year-old I'd met years earlier.

José introduced me to Bennie and Sandra, a married couple barely out of their teens, along with their 2-year-old son, Aywâstan. Bennie and Sandra were curious and friendly, and little Aywâstan (Cree for "calm") reached out to me in a touching gesture. I pulled him through the window for a hug. A few minutes later, after Bennie had promised to return in the morning to show us around, the Impala crawled off.

Back at our campsite, we found three dogs growling in the vicinity of our tent, faced off around an open food barrel. Down the shoreline, a group of kids dashed off into the night. As we drew near, one of the mutts made a bold move, burying his nose in our larder—I assumed the kids had unlatched it—and then running off toward the beach with a sack of trail mix swinging from his chops. Neither José nor I stated the obvious as we entered the tent for the night, but it did seem clear that the warning offered by "old boy racist Hap" had been prescient.

As I climbed into my sleeping bag, José reached into a white plastic grocery sack he'd carried down. He pulled out a king-sized Snickers bar and a can of Coca-Cola, popping the top with emphasis. The sweet fizz filled the enclosed space, tickling my nose, and activating in me an overpowering lust for cold bubbling liquid and blood-building sugars.

I glared at José through rabid eyes. While I was setting up camp, I thought, he was running around the rez with his new friends, acquiring junk food for himself. And the way he was reveling in its consumption felt intentionally mean-spirited.

José detected my anger and responded decisively. "I got you, bro," he said, handing the sack over. I found a can of Coke in it, along with a Snickers bar the size of my face— all compliments, José reported, of our new friends.

I feasted while lying on my sleeping bag, listening to the distant booming of thunderheads sweeping across the far end of Oxford Lake. Through the mosquito netting I could see the incandescent tops of skyscraper clouds as they ignited with internal lightning. A whooshing breeze blew up from the beach, filling the tent with chilly autumnal air scented with burning leaves, a sensory experience I was intimately familiar with from living in the Twin Cities. I had never smelled it in July, however.

Still some 200 miles from Hudson Bay, we had entered the coastal region, and for the remainder of our travels we would be subject to the unforgiving wrath of the North Atlantic climactic zone.

The following morning, the first people we saw as we came over the hill and into Oxford House were two men about José's age, leaning on the hatch of a rusty Ford pickup. One had a buzz cut and was overweight, the other was tall and thin as a poplar stalk, with a long braid down his back. They motioned with their chins for us to approach them.

"Where you guys from, hey?"

By the looks of things they were painters: T-shirts, Dickies, and steel-toed boots splattered with whitewash. But we soon learned that in fact they were unemployed construction workers—and pot dealers, offering joints for "ten loonies a pop." They explained that they worked sporadically at building sites in Thompson, northern Manitoba's regional business hub. But times were tough, and jobs hard to come by. During their frequent layoffs they flew back to Oxford House with a "load of good shit" to keep them in loonies. They spent their final paychecks on street drugs and then sold them on the reserve, turning a handsome profit. They added that while $10 for a joint might sound extreme to us, the locals were used to paying exorbitant prices for everything. When the road was closed for five months each summer, Oxford House had no land link to the outside world. But even with an unemployment rate approaching 80 percent, people paid ridiculous money for drugs.

"They got everything up there at Thompson," said the big guy. "It's like Amsterdam but with better drugs: cocaine, ecstasy, meth, hydroponic weed, oxys, heroin, opium. There ain't nothing you can't get."

"I love it up there, man," said the skinny dude. "But I also like to come home. These are my people, you know. It's beautiful here, and you can relax. Up there, it's always crazy, everyone working and getting it on. I like to come home and chill."

I stepped back from the conversation and listened to José tell them about our trip, and about his family back in Saint Paul. They spoke with the cadence and sensibility familiar to me from living and working with indigenous people across the continent. It was easy to imagine the three of them on a corner in Frogtown, making small talk while waiting for the bus.

After parting ways with the two Cree men, I turned my attention to the next phase of our trip. I figured we had 10 to 12 days of paddling between us and York Factory, and I knew we were well provisioned for a jump of that length. And yet I sensed an instinctual urge to restock before pushing into the one of the remotest stretches of river in North America.

There were two convenience stores in town, along with a branch of the Northern Store, which seemed to offer mostly processed food and dry goods to isolated communities. When we looked more closely in the Northern Store's poorly lit warehouse, most of what we found was beyond the expiration dates, and the meat in the refrigerated case was spoiled grey.

José filled our cart with cans of Beefaroni. "I can't survive out there on that goddamn bird food," he explained. However, he had no money and I refused to pay five dollars per can for food that was both expired and overpriced. I was content with subsisting on dehydrated vegetarian meals over the course of our journey to York Factory, but I added just a few Snickers bars and cans of Coke for both of us.

We stood in line at the cashier, bickering like an old married couple until I finally agreed to buy three cans of Beefaroni and two large and surprisingly inexpensive pouches of "spicy smoked meat jerky." That this mystery meat was 15 months beyond its expiration date didn't seem to concern him.

We noticed that the man from out in the harbor—the one we'd seen wearing the sparkling motorcycle helmet—was ahead of us in line. And he was still wearing the cherry-red helmet, as he would be each time we crossed paths with him that afternoon. Here in the Northern Store, the locals were unfazed by this bizarre headwear.

José couldn't contain himself as we left the store. "Bro,

did you see that? That's some eccentric shit. Who goes around in a motorcycle helmet? Nigga must be loco."

On our walk back to the campsite we saw an attractive log cabin that housed the Bunibonibee Cree Nation's Department of Natural Resources. Passing the main entrance, we found ourselves in the shadow of one of the largest men I'd ever seen. He stood in the middle of the gravel lane as if he'd been expecting us. The giant introduced himself as Silas, the nation's conservation officer. He wore a tan uniform and shook our hands with crushing aggression.

"You the canoe guys that set up camp on our land?" he asked in an accent that sounded more Quebecois than Cree.

We nodded affirmatively.

"We don't allow that," Silas explained. "There's a perfectly good beach on the other side of the river. Why you think it OK to move in over here? We don't know you and we don't need no trouble. We got plenty of trouble here already."

José and I were unsettled. Silas's physicality was overwhelming, as if he could snuff out our lives with a single stomp of his work boot.

After learning that José was "Sioux from the States," Silas eased up, grinning and praising us for our courage, and for being the rare paddlers who didn't "fly halfway up the river with their fancy gear, and then go home and tell everyone they paddled the Hayes. You guys done it right, starting at Norway House, at the beginning of our route."

Silas was ebullient, and I thought to ask him how far we

were from Hudson Bay. "It look far on the map, but from here the river really move," he replied. "The last hundred miles to the bay go so fast you can paddle it in two day or less. Before that, you got 140 miles of rapid and real danger-ous going."

Silas went on to explain that each year he saw a half dozen or so groups of canoeists pass through Oxford House. But we were the first party that summer.

He warned that polar bears and sasquatches had been sighted recently on Oxford Lake. "Our people see the sas-quatch here a lot, but it's very rare to see polar bears. Polar bear habitat is melting, though, and they're ranging south to find food." Silas paused ominously, then added, "From here on out you fellas will be traveling in polar bear terri-tory. Hope you brought your gun."

José replied in a panicked falsetto, explaining how we had come to Canada well prepared, only to have our gun stolen down near the border. Silas sought to reassure him. If we were careful to store our food properly, he explained, the only bears we were likely to see would be black bears.

I shared José's discomfort at the thought of traveling unarmed through several hundred miles of polar bear terri-tory, but I didn't say so. For the next several days, however, I would be in a heightened state of anxiety over the pos-sibility that polar bears lurked around the next river bend, poised to defend their territory.

Silas encouraged us to go inside the cabin to peruse the "free government literature" that would "help make for a safer journey." I had the clear sense that he viewed our expedition as woefully ill-equipped and undermanned.

The interior of the cabin was well appointed and comfortable, the kind of place that would make a long dark winter tolerable, even pleasant. The walls were constructed of massive logs that kept the interior cool in the summer. It was dim and airy and filled with the sweet scent of the hundreds of fires that had burned in the rock-lined fireplace. Bearskin rugs covered the smooth wooden floors and there was a loft filled with gear and boxes.

José found the Department of Natural Resources pamphlet rack. It was filled with information on preventing forest fires, no-trace camping, avoiding poisonous plants and berries, how to hang food to thwart bear attacks, and taking precautions against deer ticks. I saw José seize a pamphlet from the bottom rack, as if it were a hundred-dollar bill he'd found on the sidewalk.

As he read the pamphlet he shook his head and quavered, "Oh hell no, hell no!"

I grabbed an identical pamphlet. The flimsy little screed was titled "Knowing the Signs and Symptoms of West Nile Virus."

"Relax, bro," I said, well aware by now of the fact that José's fear of West Nile bordered on pathological.

"What are we gonna do?" he whined. "I'm gonna die out there."

I attempted to put José at ease, but everything I had to say just sent him into a deeper spiral. The symptoms

227

included in the pamphlet were worse than those he had read about previously, leading him to conclude that the woods of northern Manitoba were blanketed with swarms of killer insects. The tan paper shivered in his hands.

Silas spoke up suddenly, explaining that he needed to deal with a bear that had wandered into town and been captured in a live trap. I followed the hulking ranger to the door and turned to hold it for José. He was still back at the rack, anxious indecision etched on his brow, as if he were weighing whether he would ever go outside again.

Finally, he reached down and grabbed two or three more of the West Nile pamphlets, then scarfed up the dozen or so that remained, as if the duplicate information would provide spiritual protection against earthly threats. He jammed the papers into his pack and followed me out into the blinding daylight.

As we strolled through town, a surprising number of passing motorists pulled their rusty cars to the edge of the gravel strip to meet us. Within 200 yards of the DNR cabin, we met tribal council members, fishermen, trappers, and a traditional spiritual leader. They all seemed pleased by our expressions of appreciation for the Cree territory.

Just short of camp, we heard the Impala growl, splutter, and bang to a stop.

"Get in," said Bennie with a smile. "You got to meet Ned Flanders. You can use the church shower. I hope you don't mind cold water, cuz that's what we got here."

We knew Ned Flanders as a hyper-Christian character on

The Simpsons, but we were confused by Bennie's jovial command. We muscled open the mauled rear door and stepped in. Between Bennie and Sandra stood little Aywâstan, a grinning cherub in heavy Pampers.

José and I briefly discussed the possibility of showering. But after the previous day's brutal baptism on Oxford Lake, neither of us was in the mood for another frigid scouring.

We drove a short distance to the dilapidated church. Directly in front of it, two men—one white and one Cree—labored over a blackened engine that appeared to be beyond any hope of resurrection. The men stood, their faces and coveralls saturated with grime. They nodded as we approached, then continued wrenching the deepest cavities of their steel cadaver.

We followed Bennie and Sandra to the side of the van they were working on and stopped beside the men.

"Ned Flanders come here about 20 years ago to turn us pagans into Christians, but we turned his ass into a Cree," Bennie explained.

"This idiot thought we were all just a bunch of devil worshippers and heathens," added Sandra.

"He's lucky we didn't slice off his balls and use them for bait," Bennie offered.

"Would have," Sandra said, "except for no fish worth keeping would go for such tiny morsels."

All four of them burst out laughing.

José and I glanced at each other anxiously, and then

Sandra asked the white man if we could use the shower in the church.

"If they can get in, they're welcome to it," he replied, pointing at the church's front door. Through a window I could see objects piled to the ceiling. I could make out broken pews, coatracks, books, old coats, two-by-fours, garbage bags, clothes, and a meat locker. Taken together, these items formed a haphazard barrier.

"Jesus fucking Christ, Flanders," Bennie said with an amused tone. "When are you finally gonna pick up that goddamn mess?"

"As soon as I can get the goddamn door open," replied the man we now understood to be the minister known among the Bunibonibee Cree as Ned Flanders.

I asked Flanders about the sorry state of his church.

"Ask these guys," Flanders said, gesturing toward Bennie. "They don't think they need to be Christians any more. They made my church unusable. But no one around here seems to care. These folks are back into their old medicine ways again."

"Don't look at me," replied Sandra, throwing her hands up as if to emphasize her innocence. Bennie and the other man looked on silently.

Flanders told his friend to try and start the truck while he continued to fiddle with the motor. The van whined and roared to life, much to our amazement.

"Turns out you're good for something, Flanders," his partner joked.

The rugged treatment of this minister, and his willingness to respond with good humor, were both shocking and hilarious. The Crees appeared to blame Flanders for crimes against indigenous people dating back to the Vikings, and he absorbed the punishment with kindhearted chuckles. I couldn't help but imagine Flanders as an earnest young missionary whose love of the North, and the Cree people he'd come to serve, had transformed his own sense of god along the way.

Flanders went on to conduct a lengthy discussion with Bennie and Sandra regarding the locals they thought we should meet. Without consulting me or José, they assembled an elaborate social schedule, with enough meetings to keep us in the village for at least another week. As I listened to them, however, I knew these plans would be irrelevant. In fact, I had already resolved to leave the increasingly claustrophobic village of Oxford House as soon as possible.

Bennie and Sandra dropped us at our campsite, promising to return later that afternoon in order to introduce us to any number of local luminaries, most of whom appeared to be people the couple figured a white visitor would like to meet.

As I stuffed the tent into its sack, José asked what I was doing. "We just told Bennie and Sandra we'd go with them later to meet their people."

"We didn't tell them," I replied. "They told us." In fact, I had mentioned to our hosts that we might be downriver by the time they returned, but the comment was ignored in their excitement.

José wanted to stay in Oxford House a while. He had seen a few "dope Cree broads" around town, and he intended to spend the evening "chopping them up something nasty."

"We're not going to meet dope Indian broads if we go around with Bennie and Sandra," I explained.

José mulled over my words. "Sounds like they want us to meet a bunch of white guys." The realization overcame him like a cloud of mosquitoes.

"We could have stayed in Minnesota and met some white guys!" I added.

"Hell yeah, we could have!" José replied, and hastened to help me pack up our gear.

Soon I was tossing the canoe onto the glassy waters of Oxford Lake. We stood knee-deep in the shallows, looking up at the village. Less than 24 hours earlier, the same sight had provided an immeasurable sense of comfort. Now it felt like a trap.

THE SUICIDE ROUTE

A fter pushing out of Oxford House, we paddled straight north, to where the Hayes pooled into Back Lake. Nearly an hour later, I dipped in increasingly carefully around placid lily pads and water beetles, becoming more agitated with each passing moment, sure we had passed the river outlet. For some reason the elation of leaving Oxford House had given way to a melancholy that overcame both of us.

José was aware that we had just left the final Cree village on our route, a stop that almost surely represented his last opportunity to meet girls for a while. I tried to avoid the subject by not talking over his silent fury.

José's apathy was apparent in the limpness of his strokes. There was only a slight breeze on the bay, but I was impotent alone against it. Desperate to make progress, I turned the canoe into a wetland and began paddling up a grass-lined channel that was barely the width of the boat. A few minutes up the squiggling stream, the grasses closed in around us, emerald and impenetrable, clutching the canoe in their grip. I stood to see our way back to open water, and a few minutes later, after poling through the sulfur muskeg, we were back on the bay, paddling south along the back side of the village and then into the obvious gape of the river.

My disorientation had cost us two hours, but we quickly began to pick up the pace, heading for the killer rapids that extended over the next 140 miles of our journey. We shot the first several sets, easy slides whose snarling waters accelerated through narrow banks every few hundred yards, without stopping to scout out a safe route. Following the previous day's crossing of Oxford Lake, I was convinced José and I could navigate any dangers this river had in store.

As the rapids became increasingly difficult, I was high on adrenaline, oblivious to the lethal threat ahead. I should have scouted Knife Rapids, a half-mile leviathan I'd noticed with trepidation when I first acquired maps back in Saint Paul. But just when I should have been mindful and cautious of a previously noted hazard, I was cocky and oblivious.

Before I knew what was happening, a sideways current gripped the canoe and swept us downriver, slamming us into a boulder the size of a short bus.

"We're committed," I shouted. "Paddle!"

Overwhelming hydraulic forces raced around us, swirling and dipping. As we smashed into razor-sharp rocks, I wished I'd remembered to teach José to draw and pry, strokes he could have used to steer through this kind of maelstrom.

Even with his back to me, I could read the expression on his face. He was stunned to the verge of paralysis by the realization that we had no choice but to run blind through the rest of this minefield. The only hope we had of making it was to generate leverage through speed, staying a step ahead of the exploding waters.

"Just paddle, hard!" I screamed.

We zipped across the surface of the water, heading directly at two giant slivers of granite that were conjoined like a gleaming blade. We avoided impact at the last possible moment, jerking left into the current.

As we pounded through standing waves, giant and angry, time and distance vanished, consumed entirely by the present threat. A cold wave of fear slapped me as we approached a black hole that roared and spun across the channel. There was no way around this whirlpool or the eight-foot wall of water blasting from its epicenter.

"Fucking just paddle!" I screamed.

I lost all contact with José as he smashed into the dark wall with teeth-shattering violence. I clinched the muscles of my stomach, as if steeling myself for a sucker punch. Then I felt water jam into my frontal lobes and stream out my eyes.

An instant later, I saw we were still alive, headed for the bucolic eddy beyond the bottom swifts. Even with the protection of the canvas deck, the canoe was half-sub-merged and off-kilter from the six inches of water we had taken on. I steadied the gunwales through the churning and eased us to shore, riding a surge of exhilaration and shouting, "Fuck yeah! Oh, hell yeah!"

"What the fuck you doing?" José shouted.

At first I thought José was playing. What was there to be upset about? I shouted out again, the release of a maniac under a full moon.

José turned and glared at me. "White people," he fumed.

We tossed our gear ashore and stood waist-deep in the shallows, dumping out the saturated boat. I was perplexed by José's anger, and wondered why it had been framed in racial terms.

José went on to excoriate me: "White people think it's fun to have adrenaline rushes. Indians don't. We wake up in the morning with an adrenaline rush because we don't know how we're gonna eat. We gotta find a way to feed our brothers and sisters while our moms smoke crack, and then there's some police at the door about to put you out because the rent got smoked up."

This was a lesson I'll never forget.

As the adrenaline wore off, my hands started shaking. We camped early that evening, on a quarter-acre island of bare white shield standing in a deep pond where the river collected before doglegging east. The exposed top of this submerged dome was perhaps five inches above the level of the pool. In a rainstorm we could have been swept off. But on this night, the skies were clear.

Three hours before sundown, José fell asleep without dinner. "Fuck this shit," he said as he nodded off. "I'm going on strike."

I stayed outside and fished most of the night away. The stars cast brilliant light on the white rock, making it possible for me to watch walleye after walleye follow the lure to the shoreline. The air was still and sweet as honey, and the starlight set the pond aglow. The rock beneath me was flat and chilled. Wanting for nothing, I passed those first hours of July 4 beside a patch of moss the size of a paddle blade that bloomed upon a smear of topsoil, writing in my journal and casting for walleye.

As the sun rose ever higher in the sky the following morning, I grew impatient waiting for José to end his work stoppage. I wielded my fishing pole like a wand, hoping to restore the previous night's magic. José must have heard the zing of the reel; he wondered aloud from inside the tent, "What the hell is he up to now?"

"I'm fishing," I replied. "I caught about 10 big walleyes last night."

"Why the fuck would you do that?" he shouted disdainfully.

"Because they took my bait," I explained, failing to grasp José's state of mind.

"That's fucked up," he said. "Some serious bullshit, I ain't gonna lie."

José thought I had killed and wasted the fish, senselessly

destroying them. He had never caught a fish himself, and was unaware they could be released unharmed.

This revelation ultimately lured José from the tent. He demanded I prove my claims, then eyed me warily when the lure squiggled back to shore. He wrested the fishing pole from my grip and cast out himself.

As José reeled the bait back to the shallows, the plastic minnow disappeared in the lightning-quick jaws of a monster pike, nearly ripping the pole from his hands. After a short struggle, he dragged the thrashing fish onto the smooth white rock, his eyes glazing over like a club kid on ecstasy. He admired his catch for a moment before satisfaction turned to alarm.

"Help him!" José panicked. "He's dying!"

Surprised by his concern, I placed my boot on the thrashing pike's milky belly, and bent down to remove the hook.

"Don't crush him!" José pleaded. "Get him back in the water! Now!"

"Relax, bro," I said. "He's fine. Fish can survive out of water for a while." The pike's cheek was punctured by a single barb. I eased the hook out and set the fish back in a few inches of water. It hovered, opened its gills, and powered off into the depths, leaving a cloud of silt in its wake.

We repeated this sequence over the next few minutes. When José was satisfied that fish could be caught and released his disposition transformed, a change so dramatic that I let it wash over us both without comment.

Roughly half an hour later, José packed his gear, rolled the tent, and ate a few handfuls of trail mix. And before long we were back in the canoe, embracing another day of uncertainty. Shoving off our islet, José swung his paddle like a hundred horses.

"Hudson Bay, nigga!" he bellowed.

Once we were out on the water, I taught José how to use the draw and pry strokes. Having these in his arsenal would give him some control over the canoe in the rapids, and seemed to quell much of the anxiety that had gripped him the day before.

Not two hours after breaking camp, we approached Trout Falls, a final natural barricade between us and the 50-mile expanse of Knee Lake. Had it not been for their deep-throated rumble, I likely would have mistaken the falls for rapids, and continued in the same cavalier manner as I had on the previous day.

Before portaging the gear over an island that sloped down a 30-foot elevation drop and then returning for the canoe and a look at Trout Falls' cascading dome, I stepped into the middle of the hissing flow and stood on a spit of shield rock whose white spine rose inches above the water line.

After a brief daydream, I realized that José was standing next to me, his features locked in despondence as he sur-

veyed Trout Falls. This spell was broken when he explained
his plan for running the falls.

"Best thing to do probably is stick to the far shore," he
said. "Go through that hella nasty spot under the fallen
tree, and paddle fucking hard, so we can shoot way out over
the cliff and fly over them boulders." He pointed at the
suicide route he had devised.

Any route over that precipice would have meant sudden
death, and it took me a moment to realize that José was
serious. He still lacked the ability to discern differing levels
of risk, and the bounds of my sanity.

The portage complete, we kicked our boots up on the
gunwales and spent the early part of the afternoon bobbing
on the ripples of Knee Lake, letting a tender tail breeze
carry us toward distant islands, our eyes closed against the
high sun. Not much imagination had been required to
name Knee Lake. Its image on the map resembled a bent
leg, the lake's three bays its thigh, knee joint, and calf. The
three pieces of anatomy jogged 50 miles to the northeast
from our present location.

Floating serenely in the calf-shaped bay put José in a
reflective mood. "No one in my family gives a shit about
this trip," he offered. "You know who would have gone on
this trip? My dad. He would have come along with us."

I had known José for just a few weeks when his father died
in 2002. The kid was such a hardened character already that
I wasn't able to detect the profound state of mourning that

afflicted him for years thereafter. Not until that afternoon, paddling up Knee Lake, did I grasp the magnitude of his loss.

He let loose with a stream of memories, putting more words together in an hour than he'd spoken since we drove out of Saint Paul 33 days earlier.

"When I was in Chicago with my dad we lived in a four-plex on the South Side, deep in the ghetto," he began. "There was Latin gang members in all four apartments. The reason I never joined a gang, like all my male cousins did, was because I was born into the gang. Some people I've told think it must have been scary to live with those guys. But they were cool. Our building was safe because they were our neighbors; they protected our block. The cops didn't give a shit about us. They thought we were just a bunch of spic Mexicans. But these gang bangers would play with me, give me candy. At Christmas it was these guys who would put up the lights and nail a tree to the roof. We had the best Christmas house on the block.

"My dad was always working the angles. Like this one time there was this dope Puerto Rican broad. I was like seven and even I recognized how dope she was. My dad started going to her church, way up on the North Side, just to impress her. He even got baptized for her, went born again just to get in her pants. He was hilarious like that. I'm a lot like my dad. I look a lot like him, and his name was José, too."

"I wish I could have had a chance to meet him, bro," I replied.

"Me too. You would have liked him," José said. "And he would have liked you."

These last words affected me powerfully. I imagined José Sr. riding in the canoe, laughing with us and sharing stories about gangsters and Chicago street life. And then I felt his absence.

MEN OF THE NORTH

We had been paddling on Knee Lake for several hours when what looked to be a motorboat appeared in the distance, roughly a mile away. It swept over the water in a wide arc, homing in on our position. As the open-topped Crestliner sharpened into focus, I could make out an obese fisherman sitting on a cushioned chair above the bow.

In stark contrast to the grinning man in the fisherman's perch, a diminutive balding figure, who would soon introduce himself as Stan the Guide, maneuvered the Crestliner's outboard shaft from the stern. He cut the engine and glided to within a few feet of the canoe.

"Where are you guys going?" Stan shouted in a strikingly Canadian accent. He stepped up onto the fishing platform, rising to the same height as the seated man. I noticed hearing aids in both his ears.

"Hudson Bay, nigga!" José replied.

"You're a long ways from Hudson Bay," replied Stan, yanking the pull cord on the outboard. "I work for Knee

Lake Resort. We own campsites up and down this lake. We stock them with firewood. You're free to use them, though you should know it's been a bad year for bears."

The massive fisherman's expression remained unchanged throughout this interaction. He grinned blankly, his eyes covered by thick sunglasses.

José and I thanked Stan, silently indignant at the directive to avail ourselves of shoreline we required no invitation to use. We hadn't paddled this far to worry about private property. "That nigga thinks he can tell us where to camp, what wood to use," said José as we paddled off. "Hell no! He don't own this motherfucker."

We spent the next half hour deriding Stan and his slothful client, but quickly changed our tune when we encountered him again further up the lake, and he encouraged us to stop at the resort for a hot meal, coffee, and a shower.

"It's up this way," he said, pointing northeast to the vast wilderness. "Follow me!"

Stan twisted the tiller on the outboard's hyperdrive and sped off. We watched for what felt like an eternity, hoping to see the craft veer toward shore. But the lonely satellite vanished in the distance.

Hours later, José and I detected the resort before sighting it. First it was the hickory scent of a birch fire, then the irresistible aroma of charred steak. In spite of the fact that I had been a vegetarian for some 20 years, I paddled vigorously, salivating over the prospect of a home-cooked meal. Then, just as quickly as it had come up, a tail breeze blew away the sweet perfume. We scanned the shoreline, fearful we'd paddled past the resort.

Just as we were beginning to despair, the unmistakable throb of a twin-engine airplane emanated from behind a wall of pines lining the lake to our left. Minutes later, a red and white de Havilland Otter burst into view overhead. The graceful floatplane swept in low before slipping beneath the tree line and landing in a narrow bay just ahead.

We arrived at the floating docks in time to catch a glimpse of the sandy-haired pilot striding up a wide pathway, toward a complex of log buildings. We tied the canoe to cleats under the Otter's wing and followed him up the path.

At the center of the compound, we paused beneath a towering flagpole sporting a listless Maple Leaf. "I don't think we should be here, bro," José whispered.

"Don't worry, we were invited to dinner," I assured him, not fully grasping his apprehension.

I had flown into Canadian fishing lodges while working as a bush pilot. The Knee Lake Resort was like others I'd known, with its camp-kitchen aroma, rustic log outbuildings, and well-worn trails. I knew how things worked in this kind of place, and I understood Stan the Guide's invitation as a natural extension of our meeting on the lake.

José and I moved toward the lodge, our damp boots kicking up dust and crunching pine needles.

"For reals, dawg, we should go now," José said. "It's funna get dark."

When we arrived at the door of the employee dining hall, José placed his hand on the deer-antler handle and jerked away as if it had delivered a Taser jolt.

"You go in first," he said. "It's all white people in there."

I opened the door to find 10 rectangular tables surrounded mostly by brown-skinned indigenous men working on plates laden with T-bone steaks, and lifting large glasses sweating with icy beverages.

I found two seats at a table with two colossal Native men. We would later learn that they were relatives from the Bloodvein River Reserve, on the eastern shore of Lake Winnipeg. I heard admiration in José's voice as he whispered to me, "Them's some big Indians."

Our presence barely registered at the table, but we were noticed immediately by the servers, kind women who set before us place mats and dinnerware and plates overflowing with baked potatoes and steaming beef.

José assaulted his T-bone initially with a knife and a fork, but soon found the going too slow for his appetite. He bent over his prey, attacking the outer edges of the meat like a starving wolf, ripping it from the bone with sharp canines.

I slid my steak to José, then walked over to fill a plate at the salad bar. I returned to the table with mounds of fresh vegetables, cheese, and hard-boiled eggs, along with a glass of chilled orange juice from a dispenser. We stuffed ourselves until our bellies bulged.

Throughout dinner, none of our tablemates addressed

us with greetings or queries. As it came to a close, the hall quieted and the glassy-eyed fishing guides, pilots, and deckhands leaned back in their chairs, gulping coffee and devouring slices of chocolate cake. I detected Dakota, Cree, and Ojibwe among the murmured conversations, and another language that was entirely foreign to me, coming from the mouth of a baby-faced white man at a nearby table.

The man sported a substantial flourish of golden hair, pale freckled skin, and forearms bulging like engines of war. His incomprehensible brogue, which sounded to me like a mélange of French, Scottish, and Gaelic, had his tablemates and a couple of waitresses doubled over with laughter. Listening carefully, I discerned an occasional "shit," "fuck," and "goddamn," leading me to assume he was speaking some permutation of English.

I noticed Stan the Guide among the men cracking up at the next table. He made his way over to us, wiping a tear from his cheek and swallowing the final jag of a laughing fit.

"Can you believe that guy?" Stan asked. "Funniest guy in the North."

José and I admitted we could hardly understand a word he said.

"Yeah, it takes a little time to catch on to it. He's from Labrador, and they got their own way of talking up there. They got their own way of being, too. That guy is strong as a tractor, and he's 62 years old. Can you believe it? And still quite popular with the ladies."

We replied, but the words failed to penetrate Stan's hearing aids.

"Noticed you guys ain't made no friends yet. See these guys?" Stan asked, gesturing to the massive men at the far end of the table. "Thunder and Owen, Ojibwes from down at Bloodvein. They look like brothers—can't tell one from the other actually—but they're uncle and nephew. Not sure which one is which, to tell the truth."

Just then the man from Labrador shouted something in our direction, in a tone that seemed both aggressive and jocular.

I laughed halfheartedly, assuming he was hazing us somehow. But when I looked over at José, I saw him stiffen in response to a perceived attack.

The man noticed José's attitude and said something unclear, but amicable. "Goddamn, Jesus fucking Christ, it good, it cool, brother."

The room exploded with cheer, and most of the men around us turned their attention to José, to see how he would respond.

José turned crimson and grinned. "Goddamn, OK, I see how it is," he said beneath the roar.

The man from Labrador moved over to our table and continued telling a story in his incomprehensible dialect. "This fat fat guy . . . barf all over the place . . . pull up the rope but no fucking anchor!"

José and I laughed until it hurt along with the rest of the

crew, though I'm not sure if the story was truly funny, or if we were all just amused by his way of telling it.

Stan the Guide returned from the kitchen with clean bath towels. We followed him around the cabin compound and back toward the docks, where the canoe still rested beneath the wing of the Otter.

Stan pointed out several double-wide trailers pasted together with roofing tar: "Them are the guides' quarters."

From our vantage point on a rise above the bay, the trailers' utilitarian appearance contrasted with the beauty of the moored floatplanes, which yawned with outstretched wings on a sheet of luminous sapphire. Beyond the quarters, a number of orange school buses—used, Stan explained, to haul goods to the resort—stood like sentinels against the dark edge of camp.

The guides' quarters were rustic, but provided the men with many of the comforts of home. There were a dozen or so bedrooms, bathrooms with hot showers, laundry facilities, and central air-conditioning. There was also a lounge with a big-screen television, couches, card tables, and a full bookcase.

Stan showed us the shower stalls and departed the scene. It had been nearly two weeks since I'd last felt the soothing rush of hot water, and I stayed beneath the steaming flow until I lost track of time.

With only a towel around my waist, I emerged from the sweltering stall to find the makeshift building bustling with

Native men in their nightly rituals. Several strolled around the common areas in towels, the bleached hue of which contrasted with their sun-soaked skin. The hefty men came and went from the shower rooms and a bank of sinks, shaving and brushing their teeth, combing their hair slick against the sides of their heads, and meticulously weaving long braids.

Others sat in their bedrooms, where I could see them through open doors, readying spoons, reels, and heavy-test line, and studying maps in preparation for guiding the following day. I leaned against the laundry machines, an unnoticed observer, wondering what had become of José.

Twenty minutes later, he emerged from a cloud of steam, wearing the same filthy basketball shorts he'd worn for the past weeks. He crossed the room warily, picking a path like a shy child among relatives he's met for the first time, before coming to a stop beside me.

José went out to the canoe to retrieve our dirty laundry, and then back outside to find an inconspicuous site for our tent, an errand from which he did not return. I rested against the warm dryer, waiting for our laundry, then made my way over to the line of sinks. I marveled in the mirror at my sculpted torso. My shoulders were round and defined, my chest rock solid. At 39, I was in the best shape of my life.

I gathered armfuls of laundry from the dryer, and formed neat piles on the washing machine. As I had done for my own kids in odd laundromats across North America over the previous two decades, I folded José's tank tops and underwear, and bundled his socks into fist-sized balls.

When this work was done, I joined a group of men who had gathered in the lounge to smoke cigarettes and watch a baseball game. The dim space was lined with worn couches pushed up against wood-grain paneling. I took a vacant spot on a sofa, and quickly ascertained that the Toronto Blue Jays' ace, Roy Halladay, had held the Texas Rangers scoreless through five innings.

I acknowledged the men in the room with a quick nod, but did not interrupt their conversation. I immediately recognized three of them from the dining hall: Thunder and Owen, the hulking Anishinaabe from Bloodvein River, were planted in seats to my left, and the man from Labrador, who sat chain-smoking across from me. Beside him sat the sandy-haired bush pilot we'd seen flying the Otter, and in a shadowy corner at the opposite end of the room, a spindly middle-aged Native man relaxed with his feet on an ottoman, a smoldering pipe hanging from his lips.

The men spoke in muted tones and in their Native tongues, all of which the pilot seemed to understand well. I recognized the nasal, breathless lilt of the Ojibwe language, and the rapid-fire monosyllabic cadence of Cree.

As we all watched the baseball game, the guides made arrangements with the pilot for the following morning, timing their departures based on intuition and a lunar map they passed around. I was able to decipher the gist of this exchange, which was conducted in a mix of English, Cree, and Ojibwe.

After some time, the pilot rubbed his sunken eyes and

squinted at the television. "Well, would you look at that," he said with genuine wonder. I refocused on the baseball game, and saw that the Blue Jays' Russ Adams was rounding the bases, having pounded a two-run home run to put his team ahead in the top of the sixth.

The men quieted and focused their attention on the ball game. On the very next pitch, Reed Johnson smacked a double to deep center. And then Frank Catalanotto drove him home with a single, giving the Jays a 3-0 lead. The men let out a cheer for Canada's only Major League Baseball team.

"We need this one if we're gonna catch Boston," said Owen.

"What are we now, four games back?" asked the pilot.

"Boston lost to the Devil Rays tonight, so our boys is tied for second with the Yankees," replied John.

"Them damn Yankees," said the man from Labrador. "Never go away—fucking biting black flies."

Just then Thunder appeared, carrying a foil bundle roughly the size and shape of a football.

"What's with all the shouting?" he asked.

"Jays took the lead," replied Owen.

"Good. We need this one." Thunder flattened the aluminum on the coffee table before us, revealing a pile of golden-brown fish fillets and bright lemon wedges. The men leaned into the late-night treat, bathing the crispy walleye in juice and using their palms as plates.

"We fish all day with these fancy guys that fly in, but we

keep the best cuts for ourselves," said the tall, pipe-smoking man. He reached across and introduced himself to me as John, Cross Lake Cree First Nation.

I was familiar with Cross Lake from maps. A large reserve settlement located some 80 miles north of Lake Winnipeg and 125 miles west of Knee Lake, it was surrounded by a tangle of natural channels in the Nelson River watershed.

I stood and shook hands with John over the fish feast. As his face met the blue glow from the ball game, I considered his features. In the dark, from the way he spoke and the authority with which he held himself, I had assumed him to be an older man. But now I could see that his face was virtually lineless, while his eyes, deep and tired, looked as if they'd seen the comings and goings of generations.

"We cook the fish so it can keep for days without refrigeration," John explained, "and still be as good as the first. So good you never tire of eating it, like Moses's manna."

Chewing on a golden fillet, I was reminded of what an old Hebrew-school teacher once taught me: for 40 years, he said, the people followed Moses through the desert, never tiring of manna because it tasted like whatever they imagined.

This choice white fish was absolutely spectacular. And because it lasted several days without spoiling, this succulent walleye was the perfect trail food.

"You and I have two things in common." John spoke slow as a swirling eddy. "Our English names are the same, and we're both canoe men."

John went on to explain that his Cree name, Etchemin, meant "Canoe Man." In his youth he had traveled across Manitoba in birch canoes he built with his grandfather—hunting, fishing, trapping, and carrying goods between communities. "But one thing I never done was paddle to the coast," he added. "I never seen the coast."

I asked why he'd never followed the rivers to Hudson Bay.

"If I paddled too far that direction, I'd have to paddle back," he explained in a tone that suggested my question was naive. "The stream is too powerful. I would never see my family again."

The glow from the television flickered off the men's faces. As the action continued in Texas, they smoked, picked at the fish, and studied the lunar map.

I thought they might find it interesting to experiment with a feature on my GPS unit that calculated fishing forecasts based on location, the lunar cycle, and the current weather—brand-new technology at the time. I found the handheld device in my pack, handed it to Owen, and showed him how to scroll through the pages of the display.

The mellow giant affected the expression of a man in the thrall of critical examination. His manic thumbs pressed the arrow keys until he had looked at every page five times.

"What does it say about fishing tomorrow?" I asked.

Owen disregarded me.

"He don't know what it says about fishing," explained Thunder. "Owen don't know how to read a word of English.

He come from an Ojibwe-speaking home. They ain't got no writing for that, just talking."

"This machine's good for nothing," Owen interrupted. "I don't need no damn computer to tell me when the fish are hungry. I already know; my grandfather taught me."

Owen sounded furious, but I could tell by the way the others held back that he was sort of teasing.

Finally he let out a roar and the other men laughed, reveling in the awkward intersection of the traditional and the modern.

When their laughter subsided, the men began to file from the lounge, washed out and ready for bed. I trailed along behind them, and soon found the tent near the dock where the canoe was moored upon the black bay.

Before stepping in, I walked out onto the dock and cast my gaze to the heavens. The night sky over Knee Lake was spectacular. A hint of azure painted the western horizon like a blanket over the sleeping sun, and streaking white space dust drew contrails across an infinite field of stars. Mars pulsed red like a celestial warning light, and an aurora of amethyst danced against the glittering canvas of the Milky Way. I was soaring, energized, floating among the cosmos.

TWILIGHT OF THE GODS

After sleeping peacefully for several hours, I rose around 2:00 a.m. and found my swollen copy of *Canoeing with the Cree*. I slipped out of the tent and found my way to the dining hall, which was silent but for the buzz of fluorescent night lights and the swoosh of a cooling fan on the juice dispenser.

I found a clean glass in a stack of dishwasher trays in the kitchen, and helped myself to the orange juice. Then I walked over to one of the long tables, opened the volume, and began searching the late chapters.

I turned each damp page with scrupulous care, and, in a chapter bearing the book's title, I found Sevareid's description of his travels from Robinson Lake to Gods Lake. It was there, over the course of an evening passed at an outpost of the Hudson's Bay Company, that he first fully embraced the allure of the North.

Sevareid and Port had altered their plans to paddle the Hayes after being advised by a trapper at Playgreen Lake that the river José and I were on now was hopelessly low. Their only chance of making Hudson Bay before freeze-up, they were told, was by way of Gods Lake and Gods River. The trapper nearly sealed their fate, however, by sending the boys along with a crudely drawn and fundamentally inaccurate map.

As they diverged from the more common route to the Bay, they faced a four-day traverse of backcountry, a veritable death sentence for novices like Sevareid and Port. In fact, Sevareid would later report that the boys lost their way within a few hours of their departure from the Hayes.

> We were lost—no doubt about it. We sat and stared at each other as the sweat ran into our eyes. On our maps there showed no indication of the reedy lake which circled away before us.... Various thoughts filled my panic-stricken mind: failure of our trip ... the end of our grub ... despair at home ... searching parties. The tendency to curse myself, the north country, our own foolhardiness, was growing.

Sevareid and Port were saved when they chanced upon a pair of Cree paddlers and Ralph Butchart, the white man who had hired them. The boys had met Butchart in Norway House, where the young Scot was a clerk in the Hudson's Bay Company store. He had hired the two Cree men, Moses Gore and James Robertson, to ferry him to his new post at Gods Lake, where he was to take over as manager of the Company post.

It didn't take long for despair to give way to exultation at the boys' turn of fate.

Ralph invited us to travel along with him and his "savages" as far as his destination. . . . Bursting with joy, we flung everything into our boat and shoved off, to trail the big boat and its three occupants. And for four days after that we trailed them.

The Crees' intimate knowledge of their homeland proved to be indispensable over the coming days. The boys watched the guides closely, learning proper techniques of wilderness travel for the first time. Indeed, Sevareid wrote that traveling with the Crees was "a gorgeous experience," even if it "almost broke our backs to keep up with them."

The Crees spent their evenings making camp for their white boss and then catching small rabbits for their own meals. The three white men sat and chatted, letting the heat of "the long fire the Indians made thaw us out." Throughout this part of *Canoeing with the Cree*, Sevareid refers to Ralph as "a prince." He describes the Cree guides, who arguably saved his and Port's lives, as "savages." Conversely, based on Sevareid's own descriptions, it seems likely that Moses and James disdained the young white men.

The boys had no time to waste. It was early September, and the frigid nights offered ominous warnings of the pending freeze. Still, near the end of their third day together, Sevareid and Port could not manage to keep up with the Cree guides, who sped ahead, leaving the boys to fend for themselves.

Thirty miles from the Gods Lake Hudson's Bay Company post and Cree settlement, the boys paddled into darkness and foul weather, searching in vain for Ralph, James, and Moses. Although it was perilous, losing their guides proved to be a godsend for Sevareid and Port. Soon they would face the most remote, dangerous, and uncharted stretch of their journey—100 miles of wild water between Gods Lake and the junction of the Gods River and the Hayes. And in order to survive it, they would need every bit of the skill and intuition they developed while first finding their way to Gods Lake.

As I read Sevareid's description of this dramatic section of the boys' journey, I looked up and my spine froze from the base of my brain to my tailbone. A flesh and blood phantom sat in a dim corner of the dining hall, at a table beneath a ferocious mounted walleye. His head rested on his forearm, his eyes were open, and his face resembled the tortured surface of Mars: a chaotic mess of channels and canyons left behind when the waters ceased to flow.

When he realized that I had noticed him, the specter leapt to his feet, pushing over the heavy wooden bench upon which he had been sitting. He was a young man around 20 years old, with unruly blond locks flowing down his neck from under a baseball hat bearing the logo of the Knee Lake Resort. And whether he had been asleep with his eyes open or frozen by catatonic depression, when our eyes met, he too responded as if he had seen a ghost.

We faced each other across a landscape of lacquered knotty pine, our lungs heaving, motionless for what felt like an eternity before we both broke out laughing in embarrassment.

The young man, who would later introduce himself as Chad, looked at the clock above the kitchen entrance. "Jesus Christ," he sighed, rubbing his eyes, "is it really that late already? I have to be up in three hours, getting the tackle ready."

He explained that he'd been lying restless in bed, and decided to come up the hill for a cup of hot tea. Apparently more interested in bending a sympathetic ear than in returning to his bed of nails, Chad refilled his mug with steaming water and a fresh tea bag, and walked over to join me.

He was tan, lean, and healthy-looking in every respect, but the tortured look in his eyes suggested a rough recent past. Her name was Jenn, he said, and she was the most beautiful girl he'd ever seen. They met on his first day at Knee Lake, and while they were apart during the day—he working out on the water, she in the kitchen—they spent their nights together.

"She was like a dream come true," he said. "A dream within a dream."

Chad was from Kitchener, Ontario, a city of nearly half a million residents, located some 70 miles east of Toronto.

After high school he continued living with his parents while he went to the University of Guelph, an elite private school. He studied marine biology, but his ultimate goal was to become a fishing guide. He met a friend of the resort's owner while guiding on lakes north of Toronto. The friend was impressed with his fishing abilities, and recommended him to Knee Lake.

"These jobs are rare," Chad explained. "The guys who score them have been fishing for years—they're the best of the best, and they keep them forever."

He was the youngest guide in the history of Knee Lake Resort, he said, which inspired anger and jealousy in the local Crees, who felt they knew the waters best and deserved to work in their own territory. Chad sympathized with this point of view, but he would not relinquish his dream job.

Jenn, on the other hand, had decided the North wasn't her thing after spending no more than a month there. According to Chad, she quit her job the day before José and I arrived, said she felt isolated and bored, and caught the next floatplane to Winnipeg. He was caught completely off guard.

"What should I do?" he asked. "I need her. I feel like I have to go after her, like that's what she wants me to do, like this is some kind of test."

"You don't need her," I advised. "You survived for 21 years without her. Just stay at Knee Lake, build your reputation as a guide, and with time the pain will pass. Then you will be a man who has built a real life for himself."

Chad thought for a moment, then lifted his head. He nodded ponderously, then again with the certainty of a man who has made a decision.

We walked back to the guides' quarters, silent except for our breath and the soft padding of our boots on the trail. We said good night, and I watched as Chad was swallowed by the light coming through the open door.

I made my way down to our tent. In the narrow spaces between the eastern pines, golden rays grabbed hold like fingers. I crawled into my sleeping bag and fell asleep instantly, dreaming the sounds of guides loading boats with tackle and provisions, the false pleasantries exchanged by rich men and those whose families live on the generosity of their tips. I heard the ignition blasts of outboard motors and turboprops, and the fading buzz of machines traveling the reaches of Cree country en route to furtive fishing holes.

After an hour of sleep, the inky night dried up completely. Dragging my sleeping bag in one hand and the water pack in the other, I stumbled into the luxurious darkness of the deserted guides' quarters and crumbled onto a couch, where I rested undisturbed until late in the morning.

When I woke, I sat up cross-legged on the couch, my copy of *Canoeing with the Cree* resting on my knee. I was struck initially by the ways our experiences had been similar at this stage of the journey, recounted by Sevareid in a chapter titled "Gods Country." As I read on, however, the fundamental differences between our perspectives came to light.

In contrast to the previous evening we had spent in the

guides' quarters, Sevareid and Port passed an evening at the same juncture of the journey in the Hudson's Bay Company manager's home at Gods Lake. I cringed as I came across one particularly telling description.

> Here, as we were stretching our tired legs and warming our hands, we heard a commotion outside. Mr. Henry, the post manager, and his clerk, Ernest Barton, known as "Jock" like all company apprentices, had beached their motorboat, home from a fishing trip. They were playing a game with three Indian squaws. But what a game! Ernest and Mr. Henry, with terrible war whoops, threw huge fish at the squaws, who screamed in delight and flung them back with vigor.

I felt the cold breath of inhumanity in Sevareid's writing as he described a night reveling with Port and two other white men (Mr. Henry and Ernest Barton) in an unselfconscious celebration of their racial superiority.

"Bullet holes dotting the walls inside the house testified grimly to [Henry's] peculiar habit of letting fire whenever he chose," Sevareid writes, and "the skull of a man atop a case filled with books . . . was riddled with shots."

Ernest goes on to regale the boys with the story of how this human skull came to ornament the manager's quarters:

> "Many years ago an epidemic killed off most of the inhabitants here and all the bodies were moved to

an island somewhere in the lake. Except for the man who brought back this skull for proof, no one has ever found the island."

Sevareid seems to receive this account as a kind of folktale, but what Ernest refers to was all too real. In the mid-1700s, smallpox wiped out most of the Cree population of northern Manitoba, as it did many indigenous peoples of North America.

It had been many years since I'd read the final chapters of *Canoeing with the Cree*, and I was both shocked and embarrassed.

I closed the book and set it on a shelf among the odd collection that had been left behind by fishing guides. I had handed José a fresh copy of the paperback in the days before we left Saint Paul, and now I was overjoyed that he'd never so much as cracked it.

I stepped out of the guides' quarters and found José already wearing his wet boots. We worked together to fill our Duluth packs and haul them to the docks, then pushed off and paddled out on Knee Lake, a tender breeze at our backs.

THE CHEAT CODES FOR LIFE

When we emerged from the bay harboring Knee Lake Resort, an uncommonly beautiful day greeted us. The air was still and clear, the sun unobscured by high gauzy clouds.

Well-nourished and aided by the nearly perfect conditions, we paddled comfortably to the northeast, making easy progress. As we neared Opischikona Narrows, the tendon connecting the thigh of the lower bay to the knee-shaped middle bay, the shores of the massive lake squeezed to within 50 yards on both sides of the canoe. There was birch forest on our starboard and stunning sand dunes on our port.

Having spent an unusual amount of time apart during the layover at the resort, José and I caught up, our conversation facilitated by a vacuum of silence disturbed only by the splashing of our paddles. I told José about my visit with the guides, described the heartbroken kid in the dining hall, and recounted reading of how Sevareid and Port had been saved and then ditched by two Cree paddlers hauling a white man across their territory.

José punctuated my narrative with his customary in-sightful one-liners. "Hell yeah them Indian guides were dope," he said proudly. "The kid had his heart busted up by some broad? Live and learn," he offered, the tone of experience unmistakable. And then finally, "Them Seva-reid bitches was trying to canoe with the Cree, but the Cree wasn't even trying to canoe with them Sevareid bitches!" And yet despite these interjections, José seemed distracted.

We paddled quietly into the funnel of the narrows, be-tween the sandy shoreline and a small granite island. At one point we lifted our paddles and set them to rest simul-taneously. As we glided over a clear pool populated with walleyes, José swiveled to face me. I could see that he was working through heavy emotions, but I wasn't sure if he was headed up or down.

When he finally spoke, I was surprised to learn it was laundry that was on his mind. "No one done that for me in forever," he explained. "Clean my clothes, dry them, fold them in a sharp pile."

His mother had been too preoccupied with his younger siblings and boyfriends in recent years, or simply too drunk or tweaking, to get to a machine and do his laundry. "Where I come from, if you want to look good you stop off at Walgreens and buy a plain white T. They got a rack down there for five a pop. That's why playas always be wearing the plain white T. They want to look fresh and fitted, but ain't got no facilities at the crib."

I could hear in José's tone how moved he was by my modest gesture. I told him it was nothing, that I'd been doing laundry for my kids for more than a decade. But I felt good knowing how much it meant to him.

When we emerged from the narrows, we quickly found ourselves in a roiling tempest. The middle bay offered large swells tipped by angry whitecaps. In the face of straight-line winds out of the northwest, our most determined efforts were rendered impotent. Waves splashed over the spray deck in a long series of white explosions. I squinted into the maelstrom, unsure if the faint grey horizon line was serrated treetops or hot-tempered haze.

Then, when maximum teamwork was required simply to keep the canoe upright, José stowed his paddle. Animated by equal parts fear and frustration, I shouted, "What the fuck are you doing?"

It was too late. José had pulled on his headphones. He wailed as if summoning the gods.

I only wanted to see you laughing
In the purple rain.
Purple rain, purple rain . . .

He grabbed his paddle from its resting place along the white sidewall, leaned back on the packs, and, with waves cresting against his face, ripped off a furious air guitar solo on his paddle.

I resisted the urge to shout at him, focusing all my

energy on keeping the bow square to the waves. His royal badness performed the final riffs behind his head, then closed out the treacherous gig by waving an imaginary lighter to the sky and belting the final classic refrain by the Minnesota legend.

Though it would take us a couple hundred yards off course and expose us to treacherous side currents, I decided to make for the shelter of a chain of islands to the northeast. Without any prompting, José repurposed his axe as a paddle, pulling like a grown man. When a wave pushed us sideways to the prevailing whitecaps, José wrenched the bow into position to face the next menacing giant. Then, like an angry chorus that segues to a loving verse, we pulled into a serene pool on the leeward side of an island, and stopped between two downed pines.

Anticipating the lecture I knew better than to deliver, José explained himself: "There was no better use of my paddle out there than to air guitar the Purple Rain. You know how it is, bro, when you gotsta play the Purple Rain you gotsta play the Purple Rain. Admit it, I was inspiring you."

We both laughed. José could tell how angry I was that he'd left me to fight those killer conditions on my own, and I knew that someday we'd both find the whole episode hilarious. And so, without any further discussion, we simply agreed to move on.

Our disagreement resolved, José and I noticed that

we weren't alone. A mating pair of ducks had also sought shelter in that peaceful pocket behind the island, and were keeping an eye on the raging lake. Their sleek black, white, and green striping reminded me more of birds I'd seen in the Alaskan Arctic than any I'd known in Minnesota, prompting me to reflect on how far we were from home, and how close we were to the great expanse of the true North.

Apparently pinned down for the day, José and I maneuvered the canoe around the nearby archipelago, searching for a campsite. Lashed by high water and thick with coniferous vegetation, the low-lying islands promised a wet and prickly night.

I looked out on the open lake, in the direction we were traveling. Like an exodus of spirits from a war zone, white foam streamed in between the islands. Then, just as I was beginning to feel completely hopeless and desperate, I saw the way ahead.

Taking advantage of windbreaks to reduce resistance and to launch into the occasional eddying current that pushed us forward as if there were a tailwind, I paddled, pulling one island at a time past the bow. José soon joined me, mystified initially, then encouraged by the progress.

"Wind's blowing against us, bro," he wondered, "but you're making it be at our backs? You got the cheat codes for life, Jedi Master?"

Two hours later, we entered Maskichikwan Narrows, the

granite-choked passageway into Knee Lake's upper bay. As we passed over sunken green blocks the size of refrigerators, José turned to me. Completely earnest, he said, "Bro, I just want you to know, you saved my life."

I knew what he meant, and it was true. José probably would have been shot on the streets of Frogtown had he stayed home that summer. But I was so touched and taken off guard by his display of gratitude that I deflected it awkwardly.

"You survived because *you* have the cheat codes for life, Jedi Master."

I recognized almost immediately that while I'd simply blurted out the first words that came to mind, this too was entirely true. Just as I had used available windbreaks to enable our safe passage in the face of an intractable gale, so had José, by his own initiative, endured the overwhelming adversity of his childhood and followed a precipitous path to adulthood.

I recalled to him now what his Auntie Rita had told me one evening when I dropped him off at her dilapidated Frogtown duplex, following a New Voices meeting. When she saw us drive up, she ran outside and asked me to take her to the liquor store. I obliged, in spite of the fact that she smelled as if she'd spent the last week bathing in gin.

"José's such a good kid. So smart," she offered, unsolicited. "I remember when he wanted to go to kindergarten. It was the first day of school and he saw the other kids going to get the bus. He asked his mom to get him ready. We were sitting in the kitchen, drinking and smoking. She slapped him and told him he couldn't go." Rita went on to explain that she thought her sister acted out violently because she was embarrassed. She couldn't afford school clothes for José.

Over the years, José had filled me in on bits and pieces of his childhood, and I'd learned more as we traveled together. José had to make his own way as a kid, and help to feed his six brothers and sisters. At Heart of the Earth Survival School, founded by the American Indian Movement in 1972, he formed a relationship with his English teacher, a white man named Gordon Ferguson. Ferguson encouraged the opinionated sophomore to write for the school newspaper.

In September 2001, José's first assignment was to write about the events on Native American Day at Minneapolis City Hall. While wandering through the building he happened to meet the Anishinaabe city councilman Robert Lilligren. The only Native American on the council, Lilligren spent two hours with José, showing him around the Romanesque building and granting a sit-down interview. Armed with what he recalled as "some Pulitzer shit," José talked his way into the editor's chair.

As the summer of 2002 approached, Ferguson handed him a flyer soliciting applicants for a Native teen journalism program at *The Circle* newspaper. He had nominated José for one of three funded internships. José got the position, and soon thereafter I was assigned to mentor the 15-year-old. It was hard to believe that this was the beginning of a relationship that now had us passing through Maskichik-wan Narrows.

FROM KNEE LAKE TO WHITEMUD FALLS

ater that afternoon, we took advantage of immense open water and a raging tailwind whistling along the shores of Knee Lake's upper bay to hoist a sail—the front half of the spray deck—and cover a good number of miles. I kicked my boots up on the gunwales and rested my head against the stern plate, watching moving pictures in the altostratus while José held the sail up to receive the bracing breeze.

He tired quickly, as anyone would, but I encouraged him to keep it up. And then after we'd cruised along for a couple hours, I caught a flash, off in the distance, of what looked to be an oddly almond-shaped silver canoe. I pushed my sunglasses onto my head, but as quickly as the craft had appeared, it slipped behind a green outcropping.

The possibility of another canoe ahead of us on the route was mystifying. Everyone we'd met along the way had said we were the first canoe of the season. José didn't see the phantom craft. Acting as a human mast, his vision was blocked by the sail he held aloft.

I was obsessed by the silver canoe, convinced we would

find it around the next point. I also knew we would be foolish not to take advantage of the tailwind; a slight shift of direction on such a massive body of water could pin us down for days.

Still, in spite of the fact that several hours of daylight remained, I conceded several hours later, against my best instincts, to José's insistence that we camp for the night. He stuffed the sail into the bow, picked up his paddle, and drew the canoe toward a gradually sweeping beach.

Convinced the high clouds that had been moving over us throughout the afternoon signaled the approach of a cold front that would bring plunging temperatures, rain, and a dreaded change in wind direction, I walked the length of the beach, collecting armfuls of driftwood and brooding over José's poor judgment. Across a quarter mile of rippled sand, I watched José pitch the tent five feet from the edge of the glassy waterline. Out on the open lake, beyond the points of the cove, whitecaps marched in lockstep toward the northeast.

I spent the evening by a fire, watching the last star blotted out by a thick quilt of clouds while José snoozed inside the tent, done in by the hard day of sailing. I prepared a meal of dehydrated red beans and rice, and spooned the salty lumps into my mouth directly from the cooking pouch.

I ate with one eye on the map, seeking camaraderie in its colors and contoured lines of relief. As a dinner companion, however, the map provided no comfort. Between our

current position and York Factory were 210 miles of rapids, falls, and mostly swift water, interrupted by a narrow,
10-mile-long worm of a waterway called Swampy Lake.
As the first tendrils of the predicted cold front drifted up
my nose—smelling of damp frost and arctic moss—the
thought of plying that last wild stretch to the Bay, knowing we would be drenched and frosty throughout, made me
sick to my stomach.

Not long after retiring to the tent that night, I dreamed
I was sleeping on a waterbed. And when I woke to a red
dawn the following morning, my feet undulated to the
rhythm of waves pushing up beneath the tent.

"What the fuck, bro!" José shouted.

We bolted out of the tent and into icy water. Without
the ballast of our body weight, the tent floated like a life
raft. José danced in the surf like a panicked quarter horse,
wearing nothing but boxer shorts.

We dragged the tent up the sandy beach, far enough
from the breakers that it would not float away a second
time. Before sliding back into my wet sleeping bag, I sat at
the open screen door, looking out at the angry lake. It whistled with whitecaps that we would soon be confronting.

"What the fuck, bro," I said to myself, still angry at José
for insisting that we stop the previous afternoon, squandering the opportunity to paddle clear of the last big water on
our route. If this weather kept up, I thought, we could be
trapped on the upper bay for days.

We fought for inches that morning, paddling behind

points and across inlets in order to gain modest advantage from the determined wind. Not two hours after leaving our cove campsite we were forced to surrender, humiliated, at one of the many lunch sites maintained by the Knee Lake Resort.

I fired up our propane burner and prepared a lunch of macaroni and cheese. After a few minutes, when the water hadn't boiled because the stove's heat had all been carried off by the ripping north wind, I grew impatient.

"That water ain't ready," José warned, as I poured a luke-warm pot over cheese-encrusted noodles. His tone was aggressive, raw, bristling with intimidation.

I sealed the bag and waited the requisite four minutes for the noodles to soak up the water, then spooned a portion of the al dente mass into José's cup. He took a noodle between his teeth, bit into it, and acted as if he'd cracked an incisor, spitting and cursing and glaring at me.

Out on the water following breakfast, José and I traversed the windless harbors pushing against the northwestern shoreline with relative ease. But every mile or so, for the remainder of that afternoon, our strength and tenacity were tested as we attempted to round another scoured point. The massive rollers and blasting wind conspired to shove the bow aside, making control of the canoe nearly impossible. We would have been wise to get off the lake and save ourselves for another day.

After battling for what felt like a lifetime that morning and afternoon, just before Knee Lake would narrow into the Hayes River channel, I spotted the silver canoe again, closer this time. But somehow the wind subsided just as the elusive vessel reached the final forested point, allowing it to slide from view again. And when we reached the same location, the wind whipped up, pushing the canoe's nose around and forcing us to hunker down for the night in a nearby alcove.

I awoke the following morning as the grey layer that hung like a rain tarp over the lake was backlit by the dusky sun. I rattled the sides of the tent as I exited, and left the screen door unzipped to welcome the biting gnats who had taken shelter on the lee side of the structure.

José didn't appreciate my sense of urgency. "What the fuck, bro?"

He stumbled out of the tent and collapsed in the ashen sand by the driftwood fire I'd sparked, warming himself in the dew. He wiped the sleep from his squinting eyes and set about readying his gear and taking down the tent. It was my hope that by breaking camp early we could get a jump on the silver canoe. José was surprisingly cooperative.

As we rounded the point from which we'd been blown back the previous night, we nearly rammed an Alumacraft overloaded with unpacked camping items and personal effects. There were boxes of Cheez-Its visible, along with fishing poles, sleeping bags tied with twine, soup pots, skillets, a 10-pound sack of flour, Styrofoam coolers, fishnets, minnow buckets, rolling suitcases, a pink Hello Kitty tabletop mirror, foot-long salamis, a Silvertone acoustic guitar, a hibachi grill, a 20-pound bag of mesquite charcoal, enough lighter fluid to ignite every tree between Knee Lake and Hudson Bay, and tent poles jutting in every direction.

Wedged among this floating hoarder's paradise sat a man in a khaki sun hat and what looked to be his two teen-age daughters, casting fishing lines into the channel. Upon the precarious pyramid of unfastened artifacts pranced and pawed a pale toy poodle with a pink collar. It yelped miser-ably as we approached.

"Hush up there, Mackenzie!" commanded the man who appeared to be captaining this curious spectacle and who introduced himself as Doug.

"Where ya guys from then, eh?" Doug asked as we drifted close to his freighter. He looked down flared nos-trils at our meager belongings, which by this point in the journey amounted to nothing more than two barrels, two Duluth packs, and one map case.

Doug nodded when we told him we were from Min-nesota, pursing his mouth. It was quite clear that he looked upon us with pity.

"What are your names?" asked the older of the two girls.

"José," he replied with obvious interest.

Then the younger daughter had a fish on the line. She brought it in with one hand, netting a walleye the size of a paddle blade with the other. She gripped it by the gills, held it against the blue cover of a Harry Potter tome, pulled a treble hook from its throat with needlenose pliers, and added it to a stringer of half a dozen similarly meaty fish hanging off the side of their boat. José and I were amazed at her competence.

Doug explained that they'd flown in to Knee Lake Resort from their hometown of Winnipeg just two days ago. They had started up the lake without spending a night at the resort.

"We're off to York Factory, eh," Doug said with assurance. "Be up to the coast there in about two or three weeks, I figure."

I told Doug we expected to make it to York Factory in a week or less. He insisted we'd never make it through the "untamed bush" with our "great lack of provisions," and offered food from their supply: "How about you guys take a loaf or two, eh, and a couple of jars of beefy Bovril."

"No, thank you," I said.

José put his paddle in the water and began pulling us away from the Alumacraft and toward the end of Knee Lake. Eager to put some distance between us and this overloaded family, I turned to face forward and fell into rhythm.

After paddling hard for half an hour, we slowed to scan our approach to the rapids that demarcated Knee Lake from the Hayes. José rested his paddle and inspected his physique with obvious satisfaction, running his hands over his shoulders and biceps and tracing his "Lakota" tattoo with his forefinger.

We slid into the rapids. I could see the entire course from the line of boulders at the top, but José still whined for the entire run, his back to the bow and his paddle on his lap as I ruddered the canoe through juicy sluices.

"Why aren't we portaging?" he asked, not trying to disguise his irritation. "You tryin' to kill the playa again?"

A few minutes after passing through the first set of rapids, we arrived at what the map identified as the far more substantial Paktikonika Rapids. There was no visible portage trail at the outset, but someone had built a knee-high cairn on the right-hand shore. From travels in the Alaskan Arctic, I recognized the cairn design as nearly identical to those used by Native people of that region to mark trails across the tundra.

We beached the canoe and I pulled on a pack. I tossed the boat on my shoulders and started along the spongy trail of green tundra speckled with tiny wildflowers, well aware of the precipitous whitewater howling like a chorus of frightened children to my left.

After struggling along for nearly three-quarters of a mile, I came to a bridge made of two round logs spanning a furious creek. I stood under the considerable weight of canoe and pack, my arms tingling from blood deprivation, pondering the consequences of crossing. I put one foot on the logs and felt them roll under the pressure. I couldn't risk a sprained ankle. I bent deep at the knees and thrust the canoe off my shoulders, dropping it onto a cushion of moss. Then I pulled the canoe by its stern rope across the perilous bridge.

Heaving two barrels and a Duluth pack, José strode up

with inexplicable endurance. I lifted the canoe onto my shoulders and joined him for the last quarter mile, then dropped it in the water. José collapsed into the middle compartment, his arms bloodless and flopping. I helped him out of the pack straps and into the bow seat, then paddled us out into the major flow emerging from the rapids.

An hour or so later, after pounding through Apakisthemosi and Apithapakiticanona—lengthy, shallow sets of rapids that stripped whatever paint remained on the canoe's underbelly—we arrived on the darkening waters of Swampy Lake. Judging from its appearance on the map, and in comparison to the gargantuan lakes we'd crossed in recent days, Swampy promised no great challenge. In fact, its nine-mile length and one-mile width resembled a meaty earthworm.

The flat banks—dotted with black scrub trees sprouting from the thin-soiled Precambrian boreal forest—glided past as we made easy headway. Then, unpredictably, a vicious storm rose up ahead of us like an angry colossus.

A large white slab of shield, hardly sizable enough to be called an island, appeared off the canoe's bow just as I felt compelled to get off the water. José and I scrambled up the rock and attempted to pitch our tent, lashed mercilessly by horizontal rain and wind that threatened to rip it from our hands. Without soft earth in which to dig stakes, we chucked our belongings inside for ballast; dove in, gasping; and zipped the door tight, grateful that this rock had appeared just as the storm booted us in the teeth.

Over the next 30 hours a veritable monsoon scoured the denuded rock. I spent the afternoon writing in my journal, buffeted by the tent wall. At one point I remembered that it was my daughter Martha's birthday, and so I removed the satellite phone from its watertight case. After several failed tries, a weak signal penetrated the tempest and I heard, through sharp static and exponential echoes, Martha's excited voice. I felt as if I was calling from Mars.

The call dropped after 30 seconds, but I was able to wish her a happy birthday, and receive some wonderful news: Circus Juventus had chosen her for the lead role in *Pazzani*, their big annual show. She was on her way to a photo shoot for promotional images that would appear on billboards and city buses throughout the Twin Cities.

By the end of the day water was streaming through the saturated rain fly and pooling on the tent floor. I don't recall talking overnight, but neither of us slept much, assaulted as we were by the high-decibel clamor of the storm.

At some point during the night I developed what felt like a malarial fever, a soaking sweat with waking nightmares, accompanied by a fierce migraine. By late morning these symptoms had dissipated along with the storm, leaving in its wake a severe drop in temperature.

When José zipped open the fly, it was clear that fall had arrived in early July. I pulled the dank sleeping bag around my shoulders and picked up *Canoeing with the Cree*, hoping to find some encouragement. Separated from Sevareid and

Port by 25 miles and 76 years, José and I were on a parallel course that would merge with the boys' some 100 miles downstream from our current location. As I read chapter 13 of *Canoeing with the Cree*, titled "The Great Test," I saw this was not the only parallel. The weather turned blustery around the same stage of the boys' journey, and their string of luck, too, began to unwind.

I could hear José through the saturated tent walls, shivering and scuffling, collecting driftwood that had washed up in the storm. He grunted and growled trying to snap the unyielding wood, then sparked a lighter repeatedly in a vain attempt to ignite the waterlogged branches.

José beseeched me to come out and get a fire started. "It's freezing as fuck out here, man, help a brother out."

I left the comfort of my nylon capsule and emerged, each exhalation visible in the air, on a stunning if strikingly inhospitable landscape. Glimmering droplets covered everything, rendered in hues of silver by the graveyard glow seeping through cumulonimbus low enough to touch.

A clump of mossy branches lay stacked upon each other in a natural depression against the side of the giant boulder that was our island. No wonder José had failed to light a fire, I thought.

Inspired by a creeping sense of panic, I devised a new technique. I asked José to go through our packs and find any available dry paper. I built a tipi structure, slid our propane burner inside, and waited for José. He returned with a handful of the West Nile virus pamphlets he'd collected back at Oxford House. I wadded the paper up and jammed it between the burner and the branches.

The public health bulletins ignited and swiftly dried the driftwood, which caught and burned. Before long we had a crackling blaze, around which we spent the rest of the afternoon recovering from the glacial despondency of the long night.

"Told you them West Nile joints would save our asses, dawg," José taunted.

He tended the flames while I resumed reading *Canoeing with the Cree*. Sevareid and Port lost their way soon after reaching Gods River. Cold and hungry, the boys became "surly and irritable." And just when it seemed as if things couldn't get worse, they did. Their boat, the *Sans Souci*, began to leak badly, and an unmistakable sign of the imminent winter showed its ugly face.

As I was pouring water over the breakfast fire one morning, I saw Walt bending over and peering intently at something in the water of the river. When he beckoned to me, there was a queer look on his face.

In a quiet pool, tiny, weblike traceries of shore ice were forming.

We loaded the canoe under a macabre sky, shivering as the heat of the fire dissipated. I approached this day with trepidation. The map showed a tangled mess of whitewater ahead: Nunatonowago Rapids, Neesootakuskaywin Rapids, and Kakwa Rapids, each braiding and stretching for miles, feeding one into the next as the river cascaded toward sea level.

The last mile or so of Swampy Lake was the final stretch of still water on our route, and we paddled it lazily. Then we ripped and reattached the Velcro holding down the spray deck, and launched into what proved to be 22 miles of hair-raising paddling. The life-or-death choices that ensued—pothole after deadhead, whirlpool after chute—were simultaneously exhilarating and terrifying, and completely subjugated time. We covered these miles in under three hours, surviving good and bad decisions alike, never stopping to consider the wisdom of barreling ahead, and gaining confidence as we went.

Had the demands of the moment been less consuming, I would have taken in more of the world around us: the tapering forest, the sky expanding like open arms, meandering glacial eskers lining the banks, rapids replaced by waterfalls as the massive liquid bounty of the Red River and Hayes River watersheds sought equilibrium with the North Atlantic.

From our entry point at the headwaters of the Red River, 950 feet above sea level, to where we stopped that evening on a bare shield island surrounded by rushing whispers, the river had dropped 490 feet. It would take just three days to descend the final 460 feet to Hudson Bay.

My nerves were frayed from hours of skirting disaster, and the canoe had developed a troubling leftward list that rendered it nearly uncontrollable. I convinced myself that the canoe was fine, and, following a hasty dinner bolted down unceremoniously, turned to Sevareid in the tent that night.

Where I sought solace, I found cause for concern. One hundred and twenty miles south of York Factory, Sevareid and Port grew increasingly desperate and disoriented. Unsure of their position, they faced an unceasing series of deadly rapids in near freezing temperatures.

> There was no portage to be found and we waded and dragged the canoe until we could stand the cold water no longer. Then we crawled into the trees halfway up the cliff, out of the frosty wind which drove the rain into our faces. There we ate a can of cold beans, shivering and crouching to escape the wind. We wore the beaten looks of despair.... Our misery was complete.

Hypothermic and dangerously demoralized, the boys were in serious trouble. Then they rounded a bend, discovered a smoldering campfire, and caught up to a boat filled with indigenous paddlers.

> In the stern the father paddled, his pipe gripped between his teeth. In the bottom of the boat, at his feet, sat the squaw.... In the middle of the canoe, snuggled among sleeping bags, a stove, a tent and boxes, guns and bundles, were three little children.... In the bow

sat a girl of about sixteen. . . . Along the right bank trotted their dogs, two mongrel hounds.

The boys drew alongside the other canoe, pointed to the water flowing beneath them, and asked if it was Gods River. The Cree spoke no English, but by pointing to Sevareid's watch, they somehow communicated that in 30 minutes the boys would reach the village of Shamattawa—Cree for "fast-running water"—where the Gods River joins the Shamattawa River, the waterway that would carry them back to the Hayes and on to Hudson Bay.

Elated, the boys pushed ahead, arriving shortly at Shamattawa. They found a village populated almost entirely by Cree people, but immediately sought out the only white men there, a pair of Hudson's Bay Company employees. The fur traders "ordered Indians to carry our belongings up the hill," and then informed the exhausted Americans that they could expect to make 60 miles a day on the free-flowing Shamattawa and even better time once they were on the Hayes, a pace that would deliver them to York Factory in two days.

Light frost sparkled like diamond dust on our camp the following morning, the 10th day of July. I was coaxed outside at dawn by a ray of sunlight that illuminated the yellow dome. It was the last sign we saw of the sun over the next three days.

We broke camp in miserably cold and wet conditions, and paddled until about noon, at which time I accepted that the canoe was seriously damaged. I leapt into the water near a slab of flat shield and asked José to extend his paddle so I could pull the canoe to shore. As I hauled him through a small but swiftly spinning eddy, the paddle slipped from his fingers and José began drifting around the pool toward the main channel's violent current. I tossed the paddle in his direction, but it spun down his thighs and into the eddy. Well aware of how close we were to catastrophe, I waded out to my chest, grabbed the bow, and managed to pull José safely to shore.

I lent him my shoulder as he stumbled out of the canoe and crumpled to the flat shield we'd landed on. His lips were blue with the onset of hypothermia. I pitched the tent and zipped José into a sleeping bag. Shivering and mumbling nonsensical phrases, he pulled the down bag over his head. I joined him, climbing into my sleeping bag. We both slept like babies.

It was early evening by the time we emerged from the tent and built a fire. We cooked a bag of red beans and rice, and soon felt somewhat rejuvenated. We decided to get back on the river. Two weeks shy of the solstice, daylight would not be an issue.

I inspected the canoe and discovered an indent in the bow two fists deep. The sight of it released a sickening prickle down my spine. We had no options. I would have to attempt to hammer out the dent, risking a puncture of the hull.

I found a roundish stone and wrapped it in a T-shirt. I pounded hesitantly at first, but the rigid Royalex wouldn't give. I took a deep breath, said a quick prayer, and whacked it three, four, five, and then six times. I inspected it anew, and the canoe's nose was miraculously restored.

The evening was chilly, but pleasant compared to the past two days. We paddled for two timeless hours, running rapids almost continuously. We went about the task in workmanlike fashion—maneuvering early into deep channels, communicating with body language to avoid boulders and stumps, paddling at full power when necessary to overwhelm perilous currents, all without pausing to congratulate ourselves or engage in any kind of bravado—until we arrived at Whitemud Falls.

Here the river wrapped around a rise of shield the size of a modest suburban home, then fell 30 feet off the other side before flowing wide, brown, and fast to the treeless horizon. Maneuvering the canoe onto the rock while narrowly avoiding currents that would pull us over the falls was exceptionally nerve-racking. But because it was the only portage route available, we had no choice.

When our feet were planted and the canoe secured upon the white slab, I felt a seismic shift of consciousness. Reading the landscape downstream—the widening river with its flat churning waters, the azure subarctic sky, the flat, treeless banks—it occurred to me suddenly that we were finished with rapids, and that this portage represented deliverance from weeks of danger and uncertainty. We had arrived at the northern border of the great forest that stretched 2000 miles south to Minneapolis.

I rested on my back that night, my nerve endings stretching like tree roots into the earth, listening to the water pulverize giant blocks of granite beneath the falls. In the mists raised by the final cascade of water on its way to the sea, I felt, for perhaps the first time in my life, as if I was at home.

NEW HORIZONS

After putting in the following morning, the canoe floated along rapidly on the yawning river. With temperatures in the forties, José and I pulled on most of our clothing and cinched ourselves into the spray deck. The river was a quarter mile wide beyond Whitemud Falls, and would continue to widen as water from the surrounding region poured into it.

We let the canoe twirl on the fast water, whose color matched the brown clay of its banks. With no rapids, rocks, or fallen trees to concern us, José and I dipped our paddles casually. Throughout the morning, we took turns napping.

Early that afternoon, we beached on a muddy island to stretch our aching backs and sighted several eagle feathers scattered about. Our feet sunk inches deep into the gooey earth as we collected a handful of them, amazed by this rare blessing.

José examined half a dozen shiny black plumes, stroking the downy barbs and whispering his gratitude to the spirits in Lakota. "Wopila, Tunkashila. Wopila."

Heartened by our swift progress and nervous about

cooking on shore this deep in polar bear territory, we decided to eat lunch as we floated along past the point where the Gods River joined the Hayes. I looked longingly into the gleaming mouth of the Gods, admiring the enormous river's beauty. It was twice as wide as the Hayes at this juncture, and likely would have carried its name to the sea were the Hayes not the longer of the two.

In the Dakota language, the place where two rivers meet is called *bdote*. These are holy places. In the thousands of miles I'd paddled over the course of my lifetime, I'd crossed innumerable such confluences. Some of them—such as that of the Minnesota and Mississippi Rivers, and of the White and Missouri Rivers in South Dakota—had always affected me powerfully. Here too, at the juncture of these two major arteries, I felt the unmistakable presence of the sacred.

I found my copy of *Canoeing with the Cree*, and recalled that Sevareid and Port had spent the final night of their journey at this *bdote*. Although the author noted with excitement the smell of saltwater upon meeting the Hayes, he mostly recalled their night as miserable.

> We put up the tent and spread the ponchos and blankets directly on the clay. It was like lying on a cake of ice, but we had become so hardened and so weary that we slept. . . . Got up at 5:30 a.m. and hopped around in the freezing cold while we ate the last can of beans.

The additional flow of Gods River accelerated our progress over the balance of the afternoon. For dinner, José boiled a bag of tomato soup in the bow. The warm liquid soothed my sore throat, but could not relieve the pounding in my forehead. The brilliant diffusion of the sun against the low overcast sky was increasingly intolerable. I felt clammy and nauseous. I had suffered the occasional migraine over the past few years, but this was the first since we'd taken to the water 38 days before. I asked José to keep watch for deadheads, crawled under the spray deck, curled up on the canoe's mucky bottom, and fell asleep.

We floated along until the setting sun ignited the tiny red flowers that dominated the tundra. Although we'd been on the water for more than a dozen hours and traveled some 80 miles, the ceaseless daylight made it feel as if we'd put in half a day.

We stopped to camp that night on a lovely spit of tan gravel jutting out into a sharp bend in the river. Apologizing to José for wasting the stable weather and swift water, I erected the tent, threw in my ground pad and sleeping bag, and lay down with a black T-shirt over my face, trying to mitigate the sickening effects of the light.

Unable to fathom a conventional remedy, I asked José to bring me a stone from the river. I smoothed it over my frontal lobe, praying for relief. The stone was cool and comforting; somehow its touch eased the horror in my brain. Although the sun wouldn't set for another four hours, I slept like a baby through the long evening and night, gripping the healing stone.

The following morning, I awoke to the sound of José's boots crunching on gravel as he circled the tent. I soon realized that he was keeping watch for polar bears. "Hell no, nigga," he murmured, "I ain't even trying to get eaten by no polar bear up in here. Hell no I ain't. Fuck this, man. Fuck this."

With the wind at our backs and only 35 miles of fast-moving river between us and York Factory, I figured we would make it in five or six hours. Out on the wide river, I took a reading off the GPS, which indicated that we were making nine miles per hour. We stowed our paddles and remained bundled beneath the spray deck, twirling in the rush of water. The banks spread away with each passing mile, suggesting a limitless future.

As we traveled, José plotted the next chapter of his life. He talked about pursuing an associate degree at Minneapolis Community & Technical College, and then completing his undergraduate degree at the University of Minnesota. "Then I'm a get my law degree," he explained, "so I can defend my people from the white man's fucked-up system."

With no more than 12 miles left between us and the Bay, José commanded me to paddle to the nearest bank. Attuned to the urgency of his tone, I hammered us to shore without asking questions. As we approached the muddy bank, I wondered why José was sitting on his hands. In response to my request for help, he cried out, "I can't, dawg. It's coming out!"

We sponged up against the velvet tundra, and José reached around frantically under the deck before pulling out the first paper he touched: an obsolete map. He bounded off and crouched behind a pitiful shrub, where he remained for nearly 15 minutes.

His ordeal ended, José limped back to the canoe, yanked the deck from its Velcro fasteners, and began hauling Duluth packs onto the moss. I thought he was looking for proper sanitary supplies, so I waited in the stern. Then he unfurled the tent and declared, "Our crib for the night."

The evening was windless and balmy, and although the current had eased somewhat in the face of the North Atlantic's high tide, I knew we could reach York Factory by midnight. I reminded José that stopping early one night on Knee Lake had rendered us windbound for the next two.

"Ain't going nowhere, bro," he groaned from inside the tent. "This nigga right here is on strike till further notice."

Sensing in my bones the dismal weather the morning would bring, I offered José a generous incentive package. I would boil him a pot of soothing herbal tea for his stomachache. He could rest in his sleeping bag on the canoe's floor while I paddled. I would get him to dry land upon the slightest indication that the train was leaving the station. I would be his best friend, if only he would quit fucking around and get his ass back in the canoe. Despite these entreaties, however, José was done for the night.

During the night, I lay awake listening to a howling cold front rampage up the river valley, and feeling very small amidst the fearsome grandeur of coastal Manitoba. My skin went damp with the thought that the rough weather now rattling the tent poles would likely prevent aircraft from landing along the coast. I imagined weeks passing before the maritime clouds would part again.

At one point during the night I unsnapped the fasteners on the phone's hard-shell case and powered up the device. The unit located and latched onto a satellite. I removed the protective foam panel from the bottom of the case and found the number for Gillam Air Services scrawled on a shred of paper I had stashed there. I pressed the numbers on the dial pad, sent the call, and waited just one ring before my prayer was answered.

"Gillam Air," said a man clearly, his voice suggesting the timbre of midday. The signal faded and spiked, but I made certain he understood that we were 12 miles south of York Factory and needed a plane dispatched to the mouth of the Hayes.

"The weather on the coast is unpredictable. We'll be out to get you when we can. If you don't see us, sit tight," he said, and then the call was dropped.

At first light the following morning, on the 13th day of July, we prepared the canoe for its final epic battle. We lashed the packs and barrels to the thwarts and fastened the deck taut to the gunwales. The wind blasted upriver, sounding like paper ripping in our ears.

Out on the water, we advanced at a glacial pace against whitecaps rolling upstream. I sought cover behind several

islands on the long straightaway to the Bay, but their ta-
pered shapes only seemed to accelerate the force of the gale.
For every three strokes forward, we were blown back two.

Had these conditions prevailed any other day we would
have remained in the tent, convinced of the futility of progress. But on this day we would not be denied. Hugging the
left bank to ensure that we would not pass York Factory
and be swept out to sea, we paddled on adrenaline, with
dogged determination, all day and into the evening.

And then finally, just as I was about to give in to fatigue
and disorientation, we saw a sign posted alongside the bottom step of a staircase leading up a steep rampart. "York
Factory National Historic Site of Canada," it read. "You are
in Polar Bear Country. Beware."

We landed in the mud and dragged the boat up to a
resting place at the foot of the staircase. It was stuck solid,
but I wound a rope around the handrail, accounting for the
tide. José and I hugged like long-lost brothers.

We climbed the stairs, our knees weak from the long
struggle and weeks of sitting. Halfway up, I paused to
look down at the canoe resting on the mud below. I knew
vaguely that I had seen this scene before, but it was not
until later that night, while looking over the last chapter
of *Canoeing with the Cree* in my motel room, that I would
recall the source. A photo in Sevareid's book shows unmistakably that the boys had beached their canoe on the same
spot. The grainy black-and-white image was captioned,
"Last resting place of the *Sans Souci*."

At the time of Sevareid's visit, York Factory was still an active trade hub run by the Hudson's Bay Company. A key post in the North American fur trade, and port of entry for thousands of European immigrants who would settle central Canada by traveling in reverse the Hayes River route we had just followed, York Factory had been administered continuously, by various companies and nations, since the late 1600s. Not three decades after the boys landed at the old post, it would close for good and be named a National Historic Site of Canada.

When we reached the top step, the sun came out, the wind died, and a halcyon evening blossomed. We gazed out across a handful of decaying and apparently abandoned buildings at the unbounded expanse of Hudson Bay.

José stood by my side, awestruck. "First time I ever seen the ocean, bro," he whispered.

We strolled through the ghost town, mingling with the accumulated spirits of Indians, settlers, missionaries, traders, trappers, writers, poets, voyageurs, soldiers, hunters, craftsmen, agents, surveyors, and explorers.

We pulled on the wrought iron handles of the massive wood fort's heavy doors. They creaked open, exposing us to the musty scent of antiquity. The dim interior was illuminated by sunlight streaming through windows on the south-facing side. We wandered around like tourists, examining thousands of artifacts set randomly on shelves and tables: muskets, rusted beaver traps, telegraph sets, knotty butter churns, a beaver-fur hat of the sort that fueled the

North American economy for three centuries, lathes once employed in the preparation of York boat hulls, and the heavy iron nails that held the giants together.

Outside, we approached a tan, bearded man who was repairing a throw net in the shade of a rustic bunkhouse. In lieu of a greeting, he offered simply, "You guys must be the canoeists."

"Hell yeah we are," José replied, puffing out his chest.

"The pilot's been looking for you all day," said the man, before identifying himself as a biologist working for the Manitoba Wildlife Federation. Apparently he had arrived that morning to conduct a marine life census of the Hayes River. "Last I saw him he was visiting with Floyd, the chief factor."

I was surprised to hear that York Factory still had a factor, a title used in Sevareid's day—and for hundreds of years before that—to describe a trading post's highest-ranking official. The biologist explained that factors "had gone extinct many moons ago," but that Floyd, a Cree carpenter employed to maintain the historic site, was affectionately known as "chief factor" due to his Native heritage.

We followed the biologist along the edge of the cliff, pausing at a restored York boat. Then we trailed him across the grounds to the "Factor's Quarters," a modern cabin with large, south-facing windows. It was there that we met Floyd.

He took a break from splitting firewood to shake our hands and insist that we stay a few nights. He said that he had met many canoeists in his time at the fort, but never before had he met anyone who traveled as far as we had. The muscle-bound man promised hot showers and comfortable beds, and said we'd eat like heroes from his generous food stores, courtesy of the Canadian government.

José was down to chill with Floyd, but I declined. After all, somewhere nearby a pilot waited to airlift us to the rail line, the first leg on our long journey home.

A radio crackled inside the cabin. Floyd excused himself to respond to the transmission, then returned to say that the pilot was waiting for us at the airstrip on the opposite side of the river, and that he was eager to leave before thunderstorms rolled in from the Bay.

Floyd offered to imprint our paddles with the York Factory firebrand—a tradition among canoeists, he explained. I declined another of Floyd's generosities, incapable of imagining how we could possibly propel the canoe to the airstrip across the river without paddles. But when our biologist friend spoke up and offered us a ride across the yawning mouth of the Hayes in his boat, Floyd offered to ship the branded paddles to us in the States. It was an offer we couldn't refuse. Nor would we come to regret this decision, as the paddles arrived in the Twin Cities a few weeks later, branded with the Hudson's Bay Company mark.

I gripped Floyd's hand warmly before setting off. We had known him for less than an hour, but I felt as if I were saying goodbye to an old friend I might never see again. And then as we were parting, he promised to keep an eye on the canoe, and move it to high ground if he didn't hear from us before winter.

With mixed feelings, we tied the canoe to some hearty roots protruding several feet above the level of the water. Thinking it might well be a long time before I could return to retrieve the canoe, and with a profoundly grateful heart, I triple knotted the line, then ran a hand along its wooden gunwale.

The biologist's boat was a flat-bottomed vessel powered by two herculean outboards. After the last of our gear was loaded onto it, the boat skipped across the whitecaps rolling in from the sea. José and I gripped the handrails along the seats to keep from being tossed overboard. Drenched by icy walls of brackish water and drained by the blasting wind, José beamed nonetheless throughout the crossing.

The biologist ran his flatboat onto the mud, then helped us haul our packs up to the mossy airstrip. The pilot had been waiting, and was obviously in a hurry to take off. We shoved our equipment into the Cessna's luggage hatch, wished our new friend well, and pulled on headsets. The pilot opened his window, shouted "clear," and fired up the turboprop. We rumbled down the grass strip and the pilot eased the yoke forward, lifting the tail wheel.

Within seconds the violent shaking ceased, and we floated like astronauts in space. The pilot lowered the left wing to bank out over the open ocean. As the red sun gleamed in the Cessna's windshield, I felt a tremendous sense of peace.

Off the left wing, I could see up the winding string of the Hayes, stretching back as far as Knee Lake. Below, the Nelson River was so wide we seemed to inch across its span, even from considerable elevation. Ahead we could see lakes of every shape and size, surrounded by what appeared to be unbroken pine forest. Beyond that, somewhere in the distance, was the rail line that would carry us on the next leg of our journey home.

I remember the entire flight to Gillam as a silent, dreamy vacuum. The only sounds I recall are the words José spoke when I turned to him in the back seat, and asked for an explanation of his sublime grin. I would later learn that the ride across the river was his first in a motorboat, and that this small aircraft was the first to lift him from the earth. He would claim that his excitement over these first experiences was the source of his bliss. But he didn't say that at the time.

José looked at me through tearing eyes. And in the electronic sizzle of my headset, I heard his voice. "This is so dope, bro," he said. "This is so fucking dope."

ACKNOWLEDGMENTS

Thanks to Adam Lerner, Allison Kirby, Bunibonibee Cree Nation, Camp Menogyn, Canada Border Services Agency—Emerson, *The Circle* newspaper, Coral Moore, Daniel Slager and the Milkweed Editions team, David Greenberg, David Hreno and family, Gemma Kirby, the *Heath Ledger*, Jane Kirby, Julie Huber, Kinew, Kris Koch, Malcolm Lurie, Martha Kirby, Northwest Canoe, Norway House Cree Nation, Parks Canada, Sallie Bonamarte, and Swan Sherwood.

JON LURIE is the coauthor, with Clyde Bellecourt, of *The Thunder Before the Storm*. He has worked as a wilderness guide, as a teen adviser at a Native American journalism program, and as an editor at the *Anchorage Press* and *The Rake*. His journalism has been published in a wide range of publications including *Metro* magazine. A graduate of the MFA program in creative writing at the University of Minnesota, Lurie has taught creative writing at Macalester College and the University of Minnesota, where he currently teaches experiential learning. He serves as director of the Mother of Waters Project, a cultural outreach program that combines experiential learning with arts education, focusing on the health of Minnesota's fresh water resources. He lives on an island in the Mississippi River, in Minneapolis, Minnesota.

milkweed
editions

Founded as a nonprofit organization in 1980, Milkweed
Editions is an independent publisher. Our mission is to
identify, nurture and publish transformative literature, and
build an engaged community around it.

milkweed.org

Interior design and typesetting by Adam B. Bohannon

Typeset in Adobe Caslon